THE
JEWISH WEDDING
BOOK

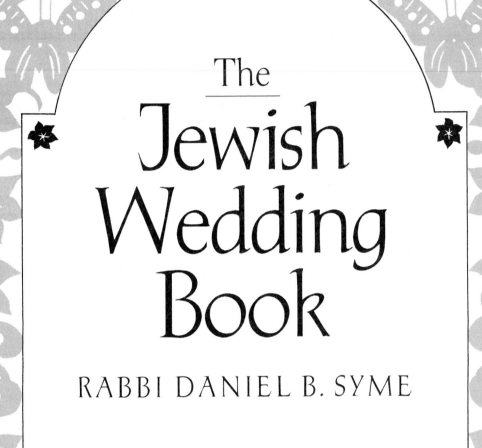

The
Jewish
Wedding
Book

RABBI DANIEL B. SYME

Pharos Books

A SCRIPPS HOWARD COMPANY • NEW YORK

Copyright © 1991 by Daniel B. Syme

All rights reserved. No part of this book
may be reproduced in any form or by any means
without permission in writing from the publisher.

First published in 1991.

Library of Congress Cataloging-in-Publication Data
Syme, Daniel B.
The Jewish wedding book/Daniel B. Syme.
p.   cm.
ISBN 0-88687-541-2: $24.95
1. Marriage customs and rites, Jewish.
2. Marriage—Religious aspects—Judaism.
I. Title
BM713.S96   1991
296.4′44—dc20
91-19995
CIP

Printed in the United States of America

Cover and interior design by Ann Gold
Photo research by Joy Weinberg

Pharos Books
A Scripps Howard Company
200 Park Avenue
New York, N.Y. 10166

10 9 8 7 6 5 4 3 2 1

If it is true that our adult Jewish identities are in largest measure the product of our childhood memories, then the greatest challenge for our generation of Jewry is to be memory makers for our children, our grandchildren, our family and our friends.

I therefore dedicate this book to Eleanor Schwartz, Executive Director of the National Federation of Temple Sisterhoods, who has devoted her life to making Jewish memories for young people and adults alike, in every land where the spirit of Judaism burns bright.

Contents

Preface

The Jewish Wedding Book came into being after many years of preparation. It is intended as a keepsake volume, a family heirloom, to be handed down from one generation to another. Within its pages you will find the origins of many historical Jewish wedding practices and explanations of their rich symbolic associations.

But this is not just another Jewish wedding book. Rather, it aims to help you place your marriage and your Jewish home within the context of the Jewish people's 4000-year existence. You will find ample room to record your celebration of rituals sanctified by generations of Jews in many lands, your memories, your photographs and your hopes for the future. One day, perhaps, your children and grandchildren will use your experience as a guide for their own lives with a pride in their Jewish heritage that you engendered.

The Jewish Wedding Book moved from concept to reality with the help of many colleagues and friends. Eleanor Schwartz, Executive Director of the National Federation of Temple Sisterhoods, urged the creation of this volume for over three years. David Hendin, Senior Vice-President of United Media, and Stuart Benick, Director of Publications for the Union of American Hebrew Congregations, believed in the project and made it possible. The magnificent illustrative material within the book is due to the diligent and devoted photo research of Joy Weinberg. Finally, as every writer knows, a book is only as good as its editor. I was uniquely blessed in this regard by the firm but gentle guidance of Eileen Schlesinger of Pharos Books.

I am deeply indebted to the distinguished lay and rabbinic leaders from all branches of Judaism who either suggested or created original material for the book: Rabbis Jack Stern, Joseph B. Glaser, Harold M. Schulweis, Stanley M. Wagner, Leon B. Fink, Herbert Bronstein, Richard G. Hirsch, M. Robert Syme, Henry F. Skirball, Roland B. Gittelsohn, Robert Schenkerman, Deborah Ruth Bronstein, Jack Riemer, Albert Friedlander, Joseph H. Ehrenkranz and Steven M. Rosman, Dr. Aaron Hendin of blessed memory, and Ms. Evely Laser Shlensky.

Another group of friends read the manuscript in various stages and made many helpful suggestions: Rabbis Bernard M. Zlotowitz, Paul Yedwab, Gary Bretton-Granatoor and Howard Laibson, Leonard and Susan Kleinman, Daniel and Joanne Weil, Elaine Merians, Margie Rothschild, Aron Hirt-Manheimer, Evely Laser Shlensky, Michael Cohn and David Hendin. To all of these men and women I extend my heartfelt thanks.

Above all, however, I am grateful to my wife Debbie and my son Joshua for their understanding and patience during the many hours required to bring this book to fruition. I offer it now as a gift to Jewish couples everywhere, with the hope that it will touch your lives with Jewish learning, feeling and inspiration.

Daniel B. Syme

Introduction: A Link in the Chain

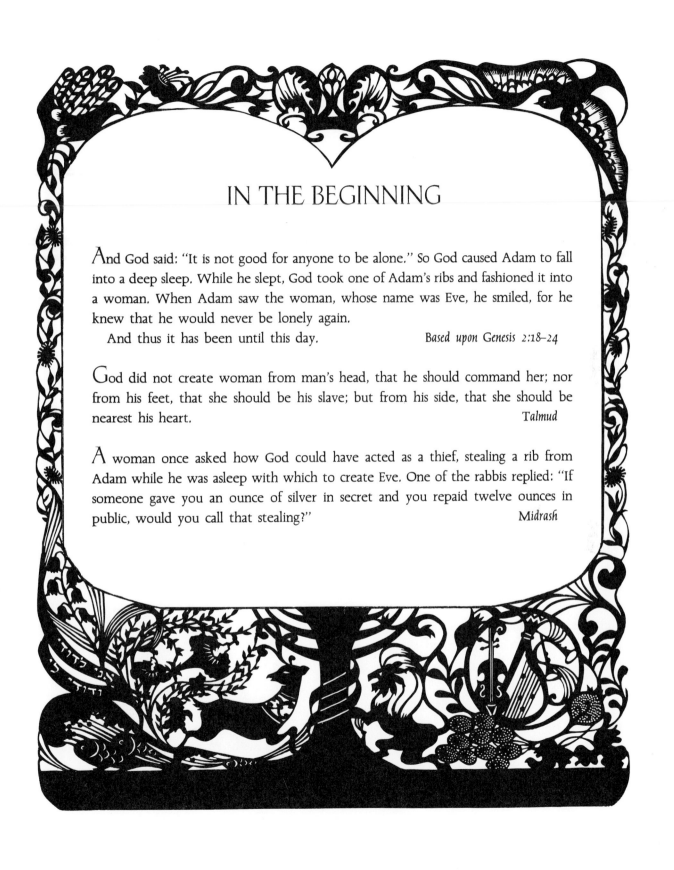

IN THE BEGINNING

And God said: "It is not good for anyone to be alone." So God caused Adam to fall into a deep sleep. While he slept, God took one of Adam's ribs and fashioned it into a woman. When Adam saw the woman, whose name was Eve, he smiled, for he knew that he would never be lonely again.

And thus it has been until this day. *Based upon Genesis 2:18–24*

God did not create woman from man's head, that he should command her; nor from his feet, that she should be his slave; but from his side, that she should be nearest his heart. *Talmud*

A woman once asked how God could have acted as a thief, stealing a rib from Adam while he was asleep with which to create Eve. One of the rabbis replied: "If someone gave you an ounce of silver in secret and you repaid twelve ounces in public, would you call that stealing?" *Midrash*

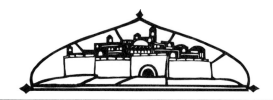

THE RABBIS SAY

A certain couple I know went to live in Israel when they were already in middle age, and for whatever reason, it didn't work out. They were ashamed to come back, so they moved to another land. In that country the wife had an affair with another man, which ended disastrously. Then they left and went back to Israel. There the husband went into business with a relative, but it didn't work out. They couldn't get along, and so they had to split up the business.

For many years the wife had been unable to become pregnant, so she came up with the idea of using a surrogate mother. She persuaded her husband to have relations with another woman, and she promised that she would then adopt the baby. The husband reluctantly agreed, and they had a child this way. And then, as so often happens in these cases, no sooner had they adopted the child than the wife became pregnant and had a child of her own. From that moment on, the wife hated the sight of the adopted child and his mother, and the husband was caught in the middle of a power struggle between them. Finally, at his wife's insistence, the man got rid of the child and his mother. He sent them away and never saw

them again. But deep down, it bothered him to have to do this.

Do you know the names of this couple? They are Abraham and Sarah. In Jewish tradition they are known as Abraham our Father and Sarah our Mother. They are the First Family in the Jewish tradition, and they are held up as the guide and model for us all.

And yet, if you were a betting person and heard this list of incidents—infidelity, infertility, bankruptcy and a blended family—you would probably have said that this was a marriage that couldn't last.

And yet, somehow it did.

What was the secret of the marriage of Abraham and Sarah? How were they able to preserve their marriage when so many of us can't? And are there any lessons in their marriage that can help us with ours?

I think there are at least two lessons that we can all learn from their marriage that can help us with our own.

The first is: they stuck it out.

Can you imagine how many times they must have been tempted to quit? When Sarah got involved with Pharaoh, would anyone have

blamed Abraham if he had left? And when Abraham got emotionally involved with Hagar, would anyone have blamed Sarah if she had walked out? And when Abraham went into business with his nephew, Lot, over his wife's objections, and the partners couldn't get along and had to break up the business, would anyone have blamed them if they had quit at this point?

And yet, they didn't. Instead, they stuck it out. They worked on themselves and they worked on their marriage, and in the end, they made a go of it.

No one's marriage is easy all the time. The road of marriage is sometimes smooth and often rocky for everyone. The truth is that every marriage, with no exceptions, has its moments of glory and its moments of boredom; its moments of joy and its moments of frustration; its moments of happiness and its moments of despair.

The only difference between the marriages that last and the ones that don't is that in the marriages that last, people make a decision to stick it out, to go the extra mile, to give it one more try, and to hang in and hold on during the rough times, because they believe that in the long run it will be worth it, and often they are right. If Abraham and Sarah had thrown in the towel and quit, if they had decided to go their separate ways, we wouldn't be here today, and there would be no Jewish people!

Perhaps what we ought to say to each other and to ourselves is: we are going to work on ourselves and we are going to work on our marriage, because, in the end, if we work at it hard enough, it will be worth it.

The second secret of the marriage of Abraham and Sarah is that they not only talked to each other, they also *listened* to each other.

When Abraham got the idea of pulling up stakes and going off to a new land, a land *whose name he didn't even know*, Sarah could have laughed. But she could hear in his voice how much it meant to him and how much he felt *called* to go, and so she didn't laugh. She didn't cut him down with a sarcastic wisecrack. Instead, she packed their bags and they went.

And later on, when Sarah's idea about having a surrogate mother and then adopting the child didn't work and Sarah insisted on driving the two of them out of the house, Abraham didn't say: "See, I told you so." Instead, he listened to her and did what she wanted.

Do you know why he gave in to her?

It was not because her *words* were so convincing. He gave in because he heard her *voice*, and he could tell by the sound of her voice how desperate she was. He realized that she simply couldn't take it much longer, that these two women and these two children simply couldn't live in the same house any longer, and so he did what she asked him to do.

Abraham and Sarah, then, listened to each other. They sensed each other's pain and heard each other's hopes and fears. They didn't always agree. They fought with each other often, but they talked and they listened.

Communication means more than just "Where's the newspaper?" or "How come my coffee's not ready yet?" Communication means "How are you?", "How are you *really?*", "Where are you hurting?" and "What can I do for you?" It means saying things like "I love you," "I need you" and "I care about you." And it means saying things like "I'm mad at you" or "You're hurting me" or "I'm scared" or "I'm lost." It means not withdrawing into a shell where you can't get hurt—but where you also can't be reached. It means opening up, sharing your pains and your strains, your fears and your hopes, your goals and your dreams with each other. If you can't do that, you may have a house, but you don't have a home; and you may have a license, but you don't have a marriage.

So, let us learn from Abraham and Sarah. Stick it out. Listen to each other. For if you do, then fifty years from now, you may be able to look back and know it was worth it.

Rabbi Jack Riemer

• 6 •

You Are a Part of History

On your wedding day, you join the sweeping panorama of Jewish history in a unique way. In a very real sense, the future of our people is now entrusted to your care. Your love for one another, given new expression through your marriage vows, makes you the newest link in a chain of tradition dating back over 5000 years.

Yours is a story that began in the Garden of Eden with the first couple, Adam and Eve. Their offspring—and your ancestors—then became nomadic bands of shepherds and farmers, insecure, never knowing what their fate might be from day to day. Your lives are interlocked with those of Abraham and Sarah, of Isaac and Rebekah, of Jacob, Leah and Rachel, ordinary people, with many strengths and many frailties, always moving forward in confronting God's challenge to be a blessing to all humankind.

Yours is the legacy of a people enslaved in Egypt for over 400 years, embracing an invisible God with a name that could not be uttered, fleeing across a barren desert with the armies of the mightiest Pharaoh in pursuit. Yours is a tale of standing at the foot of a mountain called Sinai and unconditionally accepting ten commandments, then wandering in a wilderness for forty years, awaiting permission at last to enter a promised land.

Your Jewish ancestors include monarchs such as David and Solomon. They were part of a kingdom rising to greatness, then shattered by civil war and foreign occupation, the destruction of holy sites, renewed slavery, humiliation and dispersion to foreign lands. It is a refrain of adaptation borne of fear, of preemptory expulsion from places once thought secure as homes, of relocation from one country to the next, never truly free, always in danger, subject to the whim of one petty tyrant after another. It is a saga that may help to explain the prevalence of Jews in professions such as medicine and law, in the diamond industry and a prolific presence in classical music. For these were portable professions, which could be carried from village to village, from nation to nation, at a moment's notice as history demanded.

Yours is a legacy of tragedy, of crusades and inquisitions and ultimately the Holocaust, genocide raised to the highest level of butchery by scientific technology and political ideology. At the same time, however, your heritage is rich in timeless values of family, social justice, ethics and learning. You are part of a people that considers study an obligation and enshrines education as a criterion for honor, helping in some small way to explain the number of Jewish Nobel Prize winners, totally out of proportion to our numbers in society.

You enjoy the privilege of living in an era of one of history's greatest miracles, the creation of the State of Israel, the first Jewish commonwealth in 2000 years, and yours is the responsibility to build, preserve and protect it for generations yet to come.

Above all, in spite of every obstacle, your forebears have bequeathed to you a world view of hope and not despair, a tenacious insistence that the world can be made better, that humanity can triumph over adversity, that goodness shall prevail, that decency and kindness must win out in the end.

Whatever you are today, therefore, is the cumulative product of layer upon layer of family traditions, ethnic folkways, religious practices, faith and cultural history.

On your wedding day, you become as one with a proud and noble people that has blessed the world in many ways. Its continuity is now passed down to you. Within these pages you will find images from the past, reminders of days gone by. Add to them your own images of the present, the memories and photographs of your marriage ceremony, set in the context of Jewish history.

The images of the future are yours to create as the new guarantors of creative Jewish life. May your life together bring you much love, good health and the sense of fulfillment that comes from a relationship of genuine mutual respect and commitment, and a sense of purpose as builders of a people commanded to "be a blessing."

THERE ARE THOSE WHO SAY

From every man and woman there emanates a light that reaches directly to heaven. And when two souls destined to be together find each other, their individual lights join as one, as a single shining beam issuing forth from their united spirit.

The Baal Shem Tov

Forty days before the formation of a child a voice announces in heaven: "The daughter of this couple shall one day marry the son of this couple."

Talmud

 # Meeting

Two Bodies, One Soul

A beautiful mystical Jewish legend relates that when a soul comes down from heaven, it splits into two parts, male and female. The male component enters a baby boy, the female component a baby girl. Then, asserts the legend, if they lead worthy lives, even if God has to bring them from opposite ends of the earth, they are one day reunited in marriage as a single soul dwelling in two bodies.

The legend is just that—a legend. Yet, when you think about it, you cannot escape the feeling that your relationship was more than a chance encounter. Of all the billions of people on this planet, the two of you met, fell in love, and now join together in a sacred bond of mutual commitment.

The Torah does not tell us how the majority of our ancestors met. In the Book of Genesis, of course, we see the portrayal of God as creating Eve expressly for Adam. Actually, there is a second account, which intrigues readers today as it once intrigued the great medieval commentator Rashi.

In the first chapter of Genesis, the text states, "And God created man in his image, in the image of God he created him; male and female he created them." Rashi asks: From where did the first woman come? To answer such questions was critical to the rabbis. They believed that God gave the Torah directly to Moses at Mount Sinai as an enduring divine revelation, with many "lacunae" or "gaps" left expressly for students of Torah to study and discern. Where there was a "problem" in the text, therefore, our ancient sages seized upon it as an opportunity for speculation about what really happened and what God intended.

Reading this particular verse, Rashi suggests that the first human being was a hermaphrodite, half male and half female. According to legend, the two halves split, Adam being the male and the other the female, equal to him in every way. Some commentators named her Lilith, a name today associated with the Jewish feminist movement. Adam, threatened by a woman who was his equal, drove her out of the Garden of Eden. She departed in a fury, becoming a demon whom generations of Jews to come regarded with great fear. Only after Lilith was gone did Eve come into the world as a partner subordinate to Adam.

The Torah has generated many practices and expressions that are so much a part of our everyday lives that we do not give a second thought to their origins. The question "Where is your better half?" is just one example, thought by many to derive from the story of Lilith.

The Torah also does not explain how Cain, or Adam and Eve's third son, Seth, found wives after the family left the Garden of Eden. Nor do we know the names of the women married by Noah and his three sons. We are given no

clue as to how Abraham, the first Jew, met his wife, Sarah. The only textual reference tells us that Abraham and his brother "took to themselves wives." By the time we encounter Abraham's nephew, Lot, in Sodom and Gomorrah, Lot has already married the woman destined to be turned into a pillar of salt.

Finally, however, in the twenty-fourth chapter of Genesis, we are presented with a detailed account of one way in which a marriage was arranged in ancient times. Abraham, now an elderly man, sends his servant, Eliezer, to find a wife for his son, Isaac.

Eliezer travels to the city of Nahor, where he camps by the city's well. In a sense, the well was the singles bar of antiquity. It was here that people gathered to meet and to engage in social pleasantries. And, more often than not, when the reader of Torah comes to a section that describes an individual arriving at a well, a marriage is in the offing. Such is the case with Eliezer.

Having determined that the surest sign of kindness and sensitivity would be that shown to a total stranger, he waits to see if any young woman will offer to help him water his camels. When Rebekah appears and willingly performs this kind act, Eliezer determines that his mission is complete. After both Rebekah and her family give their assent to the marriage, she returns to meet and marry Isaac.

As Eliezer, Rebekah and the servants approach Abraham's home, Rebekah spies a man walking in the field. After determining that the man is Isaac, her intended, the text records, "she took her veil and covered herself." From that day to this, it has become customary for brides to wear veils at weddings.

Not all marriages were arranged by intermediaries, however. The story of our ancestor Jacob reveals a different way of meeting and falling in love.

Jacob also met his future wife at a well. Fleeing the wrath of his brother, Esau, after stealing Esau's birthright, Jacob arrives at a place called Haran. Here his uncle Laban dwells, and here Jacob hopes he will find refuge. As did Eliezer in Nahor, Jacob seeks out the community's well, where he knows he will be able to find directions to Laban's tent. And here again, the mention of the well signals an impending engagement.

Sure enough, as Jacob nears the well at Haran, Rachel approaches with her father Laban's sheep. In what can only be characterized as "love at first sight," Jacob is so overwhelmed by Rachel's beauty that he kisses her and bursts into tears, and shortly thereafter asks for her hand in marriage. Laban exacts a price. Jacob must work for Laban for seven years, and even then he is tricked into marrying her sister Leah first. The deception of Jacob by Laban, who substitutes Leah for Rachel at the wedding ceremony, gave rise to the custom of *lifting* the bride's veil prior to the beginning of the wedding ceremony. We thus derive the *wearing* of the veil from Rebekah and the *lifting* of the veil from Jacob.

A third encounter completes a sampling of the ways in which Torah couples met. Joseph, the first-born son of Jacob's beloved Rachel and favored by his father, was hated by his brothers, who sold him into slavery. After languishing in an Egyptian prison, Joseph won his release by demonstrating his consummate skill in dream interpretation, and eventually became governor of all the land. In Egyptian society, the Pharaoh often decided who would marry whom in his royal court. Such was the case with Joseph. In the forty-first chapter of Genesis, we read that Pharaoh gave Joseph an Egyptian name and then "gave him for a wife Asenath, daughter of Poti-phera, priest of On." In other words, Joseph, a Hebrew, married the daughter of an Egyptian priest in a match ordered by Egypt's ruler. In spite of this first interreligious marriage between Jew and non-Jew in all recorded history, Joseph's sons are considered Jewish. Indeed, parents to this day bless their sons on Shabbat in these words, "May God make you as Ephraim and Manasseh."

We learn from this story that in biblical

times, children derived their Jewish status from their father, regardless of the religion of their mother. Such was the case with the sons of Joseph, and so too with the children of Judaism's greatest hero, Moses, whose wife, Zipporah, was the daughter of a Midianite priest. The custom of tracing the child's Jewish descent to the matrilineal rather than the patrilineal line emerged many centuries later, at the time of the prophet Ezra, and marked a change in historical custom.

Our biblical forebears, then, met their spouses-to-be in many different ways. Some married women they had never met prior to the formalization of the agreement to marry. Jacob pursued Rachel and remained constant in his love for her in the face of a terrible deception. Joseph and Moses married women who were not born Jewish, whom they encountered in foreign lands. In other words, there is no single way in which the miraculous chemistry of meeting is portrayed in the literature of biblical times. The wonder of meeting remains no less mysterious today.

You, too, undoubtedly cherish the memory of the day on which you first met. It may have been what you believe was a chance encounter or a product of friends' conviction that they knew exactly the right person for you. After a lifetime of growth, development and search, though, that bond of love was somehow forged, whether in an instant or over a period of years.

Love is a gift far more precious than any material object you will ever possess. Perhaps the mystics' legend has more than a grain of truth. Perhaps you have indeed found the other half of your soul, to be reunited at last on your wedding day.

THE JOURNEY

BRIDE

Grandparents   *Grandparents*

_____ _____   _____ _____
(name and country of birth)   (name and country of birth)

PHOTO   PHOTO

Parents

_____ _____
(name and country of birth)

PHOTO

You

CHILDHOOD   HIGH SCHOOL   YOUNG ADULT
PHOTO   PHOTO   PHOTO

G R O O M

Grandparents   *Grandparents*

_____ _____   _____ _____
(name and country of birth)   (name and country of birth)

PHOTO   PHOTO

Parents

_____ _____
(name and country of birth)

PHOTO

You

CHILDHOOD   HIGH SCHOOL   YOUNG ADULT
PHOTO   PHOTO   PHOTO

HOW YOU MET

Year: _____

Date: _____

Circumstances: _____

_____

_____

What made you want to see each other again? _____

_____

_____

What was your most unusual date? _____

_____

_____

How/when did you realize that you had fallen in love?

Bride: _____

_____

_____

_____

Groom: _____

_____

_____

_____

Deciding

THERE ARE THOSE WHO SAY

Find a companion, one to whom you can tell your secrets. *Mishnah*

He who wins the love of a wise woman by virtue of his own noble character has won life's greatest victory.

Zohar

It is easy to acquire an enemy but difficult to acquire a friend. *Midrash*

One who finds a faithful friend finds a treasure. *Midrash*

To love and be loved, this on earth is the highest bliss. *Heinrich Heine*

You have captured my heart, my own, my bride. You have captured my heart with one glance of your eyes....

Song of Songs

Be quick in buying land but careful in choosing a wife. *Talmud*

One heart is mirror to the other. *Jewish Folk Saying*

THERE ARE THOSE WHO SAY

MIRROR EYES

The mirror is not neutral
A cool, silver-covered surface
reflecting me impartially

It has its own shape,
its own concave, convex bent.

No two mirrors are alike
I choose one in which
to find my own image.

Some mirrors make me look
hard and gross.
However I fix my smile, it reflects
a grimace.
However wide I set my eyes,
open and accepting, it appears
a squinting meanness.

Other mirrors see me differently
and raise me up to
new confidence, new trust.

Your eyes are mirrors
and like them are not neutral.
I look in them to find myself.
I choose the eyes
which do not focus on my blemishes alone
But see the other features which compensate.

I do not choose eyes which flutter flattery
Eyes blind to flaws
But eyes which
accept my scars
as marks of suffering and growth.
Eyes which do not blink away my
crooked nose and twisted mouth
But wink encouragement and hope and love.

Rabbi Harold M. Schulweis

Bringing the Couple Together

God does not punish the shadchan [matchmaker] for telling lies.
Jewish Folk Saying

As was true in olden times, many postbiblical Jewish parents did not fully trust the ability of their children to find suitable mates on their own.

According to Jewish tradition, the successful matching of men and women in marriage is a responsibility requiring the wisdom of God, and rabbinic literature relates many instances of self-styled matchmakers who failed miserably because they doubted the difficulty of the task. Therefore, the *shadchan*, the professional matchmaker, was for many centuries one of the most colorful figures in Judaism.

During the early Middle Ages, matchmaking became a true vocation. The *shadchan* sought to arrange marriages that would please the parents of both the prospective bride and groom. As early as possible in children's lives, the *shadchan* approached both sets of parents with what seemed to him or her to be a "perfect match." The major goal of a match was compatibility; love was a secondary consideration. A good match, it was assumed, would help to engender love sometime later in life.

In a touching moment in the Broadway musical *Fiddler on the Roof*, Tevye the milkman asks his wife Golde in song: "Do you love me?" She considers the question preposterous and ticks off a long list of ways in which she has demonstrated her devotion over the twenty-five years of their marriage. But Tevye will not be deterred, repeating his question insistently: "But do you love me?" Finally, Golde responds: "I suppose I do," and Tevye echoes: "And I suppose I love you too." Thereupon, the two join in declaring "It doesn't change a thing, but after twenty-five years it's nice to know." Such was the *shtetl* view of marital love.

During the late eighteenth and early nineteenth centuries, love first became a major reason for marriage, and the role of the matchmaker diminished. To this day, however, many Jewish communities continue the practice of arranging marriages; thus, the *shadchan* is still with us.

An ideal match, or *shidduch*, had certain basic goals: similar social class, different complexions, different heights, same approximate age, and so on. The *shadchan* looked for boys and girls who possessed good character and a high degree of piety. Above all, the *shadchan* tried to match scholarship to wealth—the rabbi's son, let's say, to the daughter of a learned, wealthy merchant.

During the era of the *shadchan*, the scholar held the highest position of status in the community. Brilliant students of Talmud commanded

respect and honor from every Jew. Such a student was a real "catch." At the same time, wealth, then as now, made life more comfortable. A woman who brought wealth into the home assured the scholar of untroubled study, the possibility of many children and a measure of security. In addition, from the *shadchan's* perspective, such a *shidduch* meant a higher fee, since the charge was calculated as a percentage of the dowry.

Once the *shadchan* proposed a match and elicited a tentative expression of interest from both sets of parents, all the parties involved engaged in preliminary negotiations. Among the items discussed were the size of the dowry (the money and possessions that the bride would bring to the marriage), which set of parents would provide which household furnishings, and the date and place of the wedding. Also negotiated was the *mohar*, or bride price, which was the value in money or services that the groom paid to the bride's father for the privilege of marrying his daughter.

In Eastern Europe it was customary for the bride's parents to pledge full board (*kest*) for the groom in their home, generally for one year, so that he might pursue his talmudic studies without the need to go out and earn a living. Also included was a provision for penalty fees should one side or the other fail to fulfill its promises, and, of course, the *shadchan*'s fee.

When everyone agreed upon all the stipulations, a document known as the *tenaim* was written. The *tenaim* (literally, "conditions") date to the third century C.E., when betrothal became a legal act. The *tenaim* were preliminary to the actual betrothal.

In ancient times, signing of the *tenaim* took place one year prior to the actual wedding ceremony. Beginning in the twelfth century, when betrothal and marriage were joined, the signing of the *tenaim* was advanced to just before the wedding. The *tenaim*, having been negotiated in advance, were read aloud and signed in the presence of two witnesses. In a practice known as *kinyan* (acquisition), the groom was asked if he was prepared to accept the *tenaim*. To acknowledge his agreement, he grasped a handkerchief extended by the rabbi in the presence of two witnesses, who later signed his marriage contract. A dish was then broken by the mothers of the bride and groom, and sometimes by others present also, as a reminder of the destruction of the Temple in Jerusalem and also, undoubtedly, to ward off evil spirits. Some commentators suggest that the custom constituted a foreshadowing of the wedding ceremony itself, when a glass is broken at its conclusion, and a symbol of a time in their lives when the bride and groom will prepare their own meals on their own dishes in their new home. With the couple now formally engaged, everyone present shouted "Mazal tov!" and partook of refreshments. Liberal Jews rarely sign *tenaim* today, but the practice is followed among many Orthodox and Conservative families before the wedding begins.

Tenaim may be written in any language and executed in typed or handwritten form or in calligraphy. Many modern couples create their own text for the *tenaim* and even host special parties for family and friends, at which they are read aloud.

If you prepared *tenaim* prior to your wedding, attach the document to the second following page. If not, use the page to preserve the conditions upon which you agreed before formalizing your engagement.

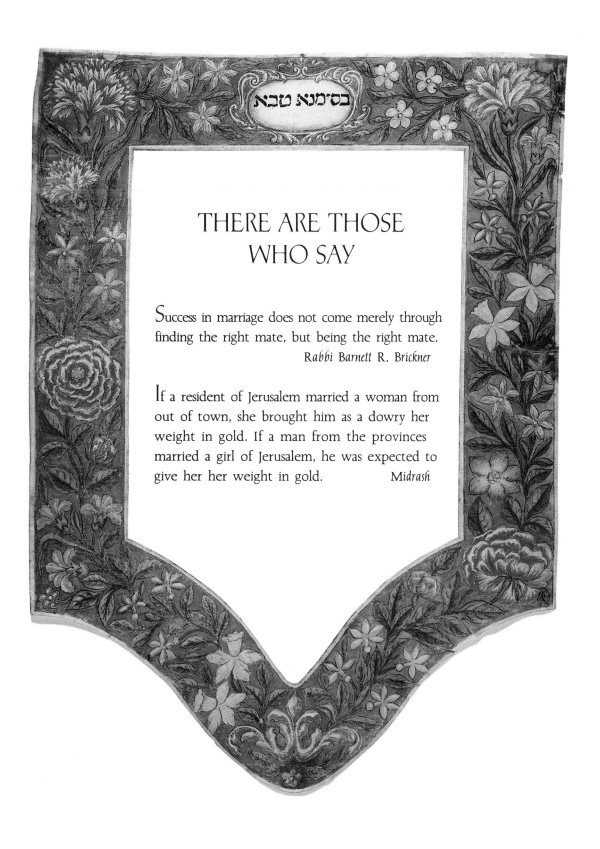

בס״מנא טבא

THERE ARE THOSE WHO SAY

Success in marriage does not come merely through finding the right mate, but being the right mate.

Rabbi Barnett R. Brickner

If a resident of Jerusalem married a woman from out of town, she brought him as a dowry her weight in gold. If a man from the provinces married a girl of Jerusalem, he was expected to give her her weight in gold. *Midrash*

OUR TENAIM

A Concern for Human Dignity

The *shadchan* arranged marriages for poor couples as well as wealthy ones. While the financial remuneration was small in such instances, the *shadchan* considered matchmaking a *mitzvah* as well as a profession. Mindful of the rabbinic teaching that "he who has no wife is not a proper man," the *shadchan* sought to guarantee that every Jew in the community would have a spouse.

The Talmud teaches that one can sell a Torah to pay for a bride's dowry, so great is the value placed on the institution of marriage. Accordingly, a poor woman's dowry was often provided by the community. A single Jew or a group of Jews made anonymous contributions to a special fund to avoid any embarrassment to the bride. This was a clear demonstration of the value that Judaism attaches to the dignity of every individual.

If you are like most couples, a *shadchan* was not part of your decision to get married. Perhaps the proposal came from the groom during a romantic dinner. Or perhaps, as is increasingly common in modern times, the bride posed the question in an equally tender setting. On the other hand, your proposal of marriage may have occurred in a somewhat unusual way. Retell your story on the page that follows.

OUR PROPOSAL
OF MARRIAGE

Year: _____

Date: _____

Circumstances: _____

_____

_____

_____

_____

_____

WHAT I REMEMBER MOST

Bride: _____

_____

_____

_____

_____

Groom: _____

_____

_____

_____

_____

Engagement photograph of Abe and Bessie Fedman Blend, 1913.

Getting
Ready

The Engagement Period

Becoming engaged is a relatively simple process today. One person asks, the other accepts, and that's that. If difficulties arise, the engagement can be broken off, with no legal ramifications.

In former times, however, betrothal constituted far more of a commitment, akin to a binding contract, much less susceptible to a change of heart, and highly structured in terms of expected preliminary procedures and behavior.

For example, in North America just a few decades ago, a man proposing marriage customarily knelt before his intended, ring in hand, to ask the woman to accept him. Assuming an affirmative response, the man approached his future father-in-law to request his permission and his blessing. A mild interrogation often ensued, with the bride's father seeking assurance that the man's income could adequately support a family and that his commitment to the marriage was genuine. Any subsequent dissolution of the engagement was deemed almost scandalous, and grist for the community's gossip mill.

This series of customs, so common just a brief time ago, may seem strange and rather old-fashioned to many of us today. The gap between *ancient* Jewish customs relating to engagement and those of the modern period, therefore, will surely surprise us even more.

Close to 2000 years ago, Judaism, too, had a two-step progression consisting of betrothal (*erusin*) and marriage (*nissuin*). Imagine yourself in your middle to late teenage years, your fiance having been selected by your parents based upon their sense of who would be best for you. Since the Talmud prescribes eighteen as the ideal age for marriage, your marital destiny was usually determined by the time you were sixteen. Sometimes you knew your future spouse. More often than not, you had no more than a casual acquaintance with one another. No matter. Romantic love played virtually no part in the betrothal negotiations. Compatibility was essential. Love could follow—some day.

Once you were informed of your parents' decision and had been introduced to your future life partner, your betrothal became formalized through a ceremony called *erusin*. A usual one-year waiting period then began, separating the betrothal from the actual wedding ceremony. Once engaged, you could not be alone with your fiance for any reason until the wedding day. Breaking off the engagement required a formal Jewish divorce proceeding and thus was not a step to be taken lightly.

In short, Jewish law made it difficult to get married. Engagement and marriage were not spontaneous acts, and agreements were never formalized without the most careful consideration of criteria articulated in the Torah, Talmud and other rabbinic writings.

Certain matches were absolutely forbidden; among them:

- Between blood relatives (Torah)
- Between a *Kohen* (a descendant of the biblical priestly class) and a widow, divorcee or woman of ill repute (Torah)
- Between a man and woman once married to each other, then married to others and divorced again (Torah)
- Between a man and his wife's sister during his wife's lifetime, even after a divorce (Torah)
- Between minors: boys under the age of thirteen, girls under the age of twelve (Talmud)
- Between a woman and the man who represented her in her divorce proceedings (Talmud)
- Between a woman and the only witness to her husband's death (Talmud)

These and many other taboos provided clear parameters within which potential marriages could be considered. The rabbis then offered guidance as to how to evaluate a possible spouse, casting their counsel in the language of the male-oriented society in which they lived.

Though some of their advice is clearly inappropriate today, much of it is as wise now as it was centuries ago.

- Marry the daughter of a learned man.
- Marry a woman of the same age or about the same age.
- Marry a woman of the same or lower social class.

אױף אײן וואָג־שאָל די סאטניאַ,
אױף דער אַנדערער אַ חתן.
— זאָג, אַ שענע ליעבע מײדעל,
וואָס וואָלסטו געראַסען ? ...

לשנה טובה תכתם

- Marry a woman of a different complexion, lest the children be too pale or too dark.
- Marry a woman of a different height, lest the children be too tall or too short.
- Don't marry for money.

Still, for all their rationality, the rabbis occasionally displayed a glimmer of the romantic. For, after listing their detailed guidelines, they then say: "A woman who has beautiful eyes needs no further recommendation."

MEMORIES OF
OUR ENGAGEMENT

We became engaged on _____
                                    (Date)

in _____ _____ at _____
            (City)   (State)   (Place)

_____

We were engaged for a period of _____ before we were married.
                                    (months)

FOR THE BRIDE

The moments I remember most vividly about our engagement period are:

_____
_____
_____
_____
_____
_____
_____

FOR THE GROOM

The moments I remember most vividly about our engagement period are:

_____
_____
_____
_____
_____
_____
_____

Setting the Date

Planning a wedding in times past was far less complicated and tumultuous than it is today. In fact, most details of the ceremony were decided upon by the couple's parents on behalf of their teenage children as part of the prebetrothal agreement.

For those who follow the rhythms of the Jewish calendar, however, setting the date for the wedding was—and is—a challenge. Jewish law forbids marriage ceremonies at certain times:

• *On Shabbat.* This is an obvious taboo, since a wedding involves the writing of a marriage document, travel to and from the ceremony, and the work involved in setting up for the ceremony and party, not to mention cooking. All are forbidden on Shabbat, according to Halacha.

  In addition, Shabbat is considered a day of joy, and Jewish law declares that "One should not combine one time of rejoicing with another." *Simchas,* joyous occasions, are precious, and Jewish tradition affirms that each such moment, a wedding as an example par excellence, should be savored on its own.

• *On major festivals and fast days.* This category includes Passover, Shavuot and Sukot, Rosh Hashanah and Yom Kippur.

• *During the forty-nine days between the second night of Pesach and the beginning of Shavuot, with the exception of Lag Ba'omer, the thirty-third day.* This time, called "the Omer period" for ancient agricultural reasons, is forbidden as a time for weddings, primarily because it falls during a time of great tragedies in Jewish history. It was during these weeks that the Crusades occurred. There was also a terrible plague that descended upon the school of the Jewish sage Rabbi Akiba during this period. Hundreds of Akiba's students succumbed to the disease, which miraculously lifted on the thirty-third day of the Omer, today called Lag B'Omer, or the "Scholar's Festival." This day was exempted from the prohibition against weddings and has become a very popular date for ceremonies, especially in modern Israel.

• *The period between two somber fast days during summer months, the 17th of Tammuz and the 9th of Av (Tisha B'Av), which commemorates the destruction of the Temple in Jerusalem and, some say, the Jews' expulsion from Spain in 1492.*

After eliminating all these dates, the couple then sought to schedule the ceremony on a day considered lucky in their era and country. For example, German Jews liked to marry under a full moon, Spanish Jews under a new moon. Many Jewish communities favored a wedding during the first half of the month, when the moon increases in size, seeing it as an omen of fortune, luck and fertility.

The season, too, was important. The lyrical biblical book, the Song of Songs, glorifies spring in particular as a time when "winter is past, the rain is over and gone. The flowers appear on the earth, the time of singing has come, and the voice of the turtledove is heard in our land. The fig tree puts forth its figs, and the vines are in blossom; they give forth fragrance. Arise, my love, my fair one, and come away."

Certain days of the week were also considered particularly desirable for marriages. Fridays were special favorites, inasmuch as they fell close to Shabbat, when having sexual relations with one's spouse was considered a double *mitzvah*. Virgins were most often wed on Friday,

ideally after Tisha B'Av, Shavuot or Yom Kippur. Tuesdays and Thursdays were commonly wedding days for widows and divorcees, while Mondays and Wednesdays generally came to be regarded as unlucky times, though the Talmud mentions Sundays and Wednesdays as good wedding days for virgins. Some modern Orthodox Jews opt to marry on Tuesday, since it corresponds to the biblical day of creation, which God twice "pronounces" to be good.

Today, Saturday night (after Shabbat has ended) and Sunday have become the most popular times for weddings, mostly because they fall during the weekend, when family and friends can all be present.

OUR WEDDING DATE

How we picked our wedding date

_____

_____

_____

_____

_____

_____

_____

_____

_____

_____

_____

_____

_____

_____

_____

_____

_____

_____

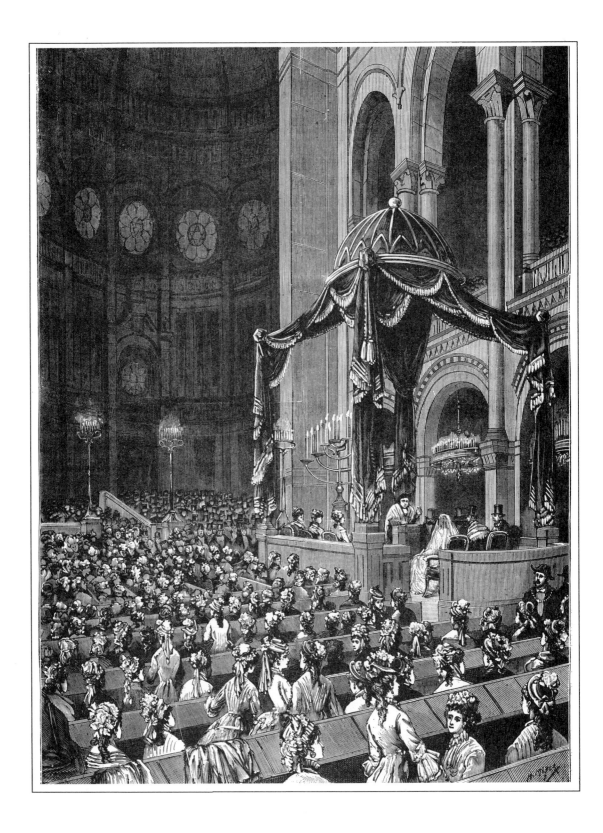

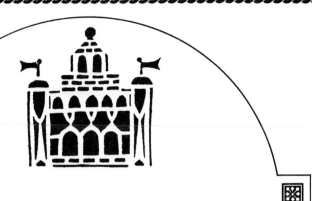

Plans and Preparations

Where to Hold the Ceremony

There is no limit to the creativity of couples in selecting a site for their wedding ceremony, and virtually every rabbi has his or her own favorite account of "my most unusual wedding."

One couple decided to have themselves declared husband and wife precisely at the moment when Neil Armstrong set foot on the moon. Accordingly, the rabbi and guests sat in front of a television set in a house until the early hours of that historic morning, bleary-eyed by the time the wedding vows were finally concluded.

A second couple traveled to Nepal for their ceremony along with the rabbi and their respective families, negotiated their way to the top of a particularly rugged mountain peak, and then declared their vows in an awe-inspiring natural setting.

A third couple selected an isolated pastoral setting in the Massachusetts countryside, erected a tent to guard against the elements, and scheduled the ceremony to begin a half hour before sunset. Unfortunately, a number of family members lost their way on the winding roads leading to the site and arrived an hour late. By that time the sun had already disappeared and the wedding was conducted in pitch-black darkness, with selected guests taking turns striking wooden matches so that the rabbi could read and chant the appropriate blessings.

A fourth couple chose to be married in the Jewish camp where they had met as teenagers. The entire population of the camp was invited, and formed a camp choir that serenaded the bride and groom with the songs they had loved most during their own camping days.

A fifth couple opted for a black tie affair at a New York City automat. As guests arrived, they were given rolls of quarters, to be used after the ceremony to select the wedding meal of their choice.

To be sure, each of these examples was unusual and out of the ordinary, but somehow they met the need of a particular bride and groom to make their wedding day memorable. Looking back in history, we find that Jewish couples most often limited their choice of wedding locales to less exotic places. Ashkenazic (Eastern European) and Sephardic (Oriental) Jews historically differed in their favored sites for weddings. The Ashkenazim generally held their weddings outdoors and in the evening, primarily as an expression of the hope that, even as the descendants of Abraham were to be "as numerous as the stars of the heavens" (Genesis 22:17), so the union would be blessed with many children. An outdoor setting also militated against public displays of less than dignified behavior. Sephardic Jews, on the other hand, usually held their weddings indoors, most often

THERE ARE THOSE WHO SAY

Our joy is greatest when our family is with us.
Rabbi Solomon B. Freehof

Friends are people you don't count on one hand; you count them on one heart.

Rabbi Maurice Davis

in the synagogue. North American Jewry generally follows Sephardic practice, while modern Israeli weddings tend to follow Ashkenazi custom.

A wedding may be held almost anywhere. Some couples prefer a synagogue, others a house or apartment. Some couples opt for a hotel, while others select a beautiful outdoor setting. The place, therefore, is a matter of personal choice. The ceremony itself, and a relationship that deepens and strengthens with every passing year, are the chief concerns of Jewish tradition.

THERE ARE THOSE WHO SAY

I chose to be married at home because our family home was the most sincerely religious place I knew. It was a place of living Jewish values. Not that it was without strife, for it was fully human. But the anger was transitory, and love formed the abiding canopy of our dwelling place. Jewish values were conveyed in our home through speech and deeds. *Tzedakah* (charity) was a pervasive theme. My sister and I learned of its meaning during dinner conversations and were constant witnesses to the central role it played in our parents' lives.

Our home was more than a place of love and learning. It was a launching pad, a place from which we carried our Jewish values out into the world, where they were sorely needed. We understood that we were Jews, not simply for our own joy and enhancement—although surely for that—but also for the sake of the world. Abraham Joshua Heschel has written that "Religion becomes sinful when it begins to advocate the segregation of God, to forget that the true sanctuary has no walls." Thus my father went off to raise money to bring oppressed Jewish refugees out of Eastern Europe to the Promised Land; my mother immersed herself in the work of Hadassah and the temple sisterhood; and my sister and I made and sold little molded animals to benefit children with tuberculosis.

I love the thought of the home as a sanctuary without walls, or at least as a place with walls that are permeable to the outside. The wedding *chupah*, which symbolizes the home, stands as a perfect representation of a house that offers shelter yet remains open to the world, to take in the pleasure and pain of humanity, to reach out to embrace and to heal.

Under the *chupah*, the *ketubah*, the wedding covenant, is presented. That covenant between husband and wife can be understood as a reflection of the larger covenant between God and Israel. The Jewish home then becomes a microcosm, a sort of experiment in the creation of a place reflective of the Jewish vision that imagines a society steeped in kindness, justice and peace. That which one hopes to foster in the larger community one works toward also in the intimacy of one's own abode.

Such complex creations cannot be undertaken alone. Psalm 127 alludes to the essential partnership between God and people if a home is actually to be brought into being. So, too, God and the Jewish people became partners at Sinai in the task of creating a holier world. The covenant into which you now enter extends the notion of partnership to you. As you wed world to world and heart to heart, you become bearers of the Jewish dream. I pray that you will carry that dream forward by working together to sanctify both your home and your world through deeds of loving kindness. May this be God's will and may it be your own.

Evely Laser Shlensky

THE PLACE WHERE
WE HELD OUR WEDDING

Name of the place _____

Location _____

Why we chose it _____

_____

_____

_____

_____

_____

_____

_____

_____

_____

_____

_____

_____

_____

_____

_____

_____

_____

The Invitation

Jewish tradition does not prescribe the form or language for a wedding invitation. In times past, a public announcement often welcomed the entire community to the joyous event. In more recent centuries, guests were often invited orally or by a simple written note.

The wedding invitation of today has become far more elaborate as high-technology printing has made possible the mass duplication of detailed calligraphy, Hebrew lettering and full-color artwork. As a result, some couples have begun to commission Jewish artists to create their wedding invitations with designs reflecting Jewish themes, while others simply select an invitation from among the printer's sample designs.

Since the establishment of the State of Israel in 1948, and the explosion of Jewish identity affirmation following the 1967 Six Day War, many Jewish practices, including the format and substance of wedding invitations, have begun to reflect a strong Israeli influence.

For example, it is now common for wedding invitations to be printed in both Hebrew and English. The date of the ceremony is frequently presented in the context of both the secular and the Hebrew calendars. Biblical quotations often adorn the invitation, drawn from the Song of Songs, Judaism's love poem par excellence, or other biblical or rabbinic sources dealing with love, commitment, caring and joy. And growing numbers of invitations even specify the wedding date in terms of the number of years since the creation of the State of Israel.

One couple decided to make their wedding invitation a vehicle for observing the *mitzvah* of *tzedakah* and for building the State of Israel through the Jewish National Fund (JNF) which plants trees, clears land, builds parks and roads in Israel, and shares Israel's agricultural technology with some fifty countries throughout the world. Rather than printing a formal invitation, the bride and groom planted trees in Israel in honor of their guests and then mailed the colorful JNF certificate to each of them, with details of the ceremony printed on the back. Thus, as they began their lives together, the couple established the beginnings of their own forest in Israel, to grow with each passing year.

To be sure, not all Jewish wedding invitations are rooted in Jewish sources or themes. Many other creative approaches are possible. If yours is a second marriage, you may have chosen to ask your children to design your invitation. Or the invitation may include photographs of your parents and grandparents on their wedding days, thereby linking the bride and groom to the past and to the future.

Whatever your decision, preserve your wedding invitation here as a memento of a time in your lives when you asked those nearest and dearest to you to join in sharing your declaration of love for one another.

OUR WEDDING INVITATION

Deciding What to Wear

Jewish tradition teaches that all past sins of a bride and groom are forgiven as they begin their new life together. Accordingly, both the bride and the groom historically wore white as a symbol of purity. The bride's garb was a white or off-white dress, while Ashkenazic grooms wore a *kittel* (a sort of white robe). This *kittel* was also often the garment in which the groom would one day be buried, and therefore symbolized not only purity and joy, but mortality as well.

In ancient Greece, in addition to white garments, both bride and groom wore garlands and wreaths. To this day, some Sephardic couples don wreaths of bitter olive leaves as a reminder of the destruction of the Temple in Jerusalem, while some brides wear garlands of fragrant myrtle. In addition, both Sephardic and Ashkenazic grooms often wear a *tallit*, a wedding gift from the bride or her parents.

In times past, the groom also gave the bride gifts such as a *siddur* (prayer book), a wedding veil, fine combs and a gold engagement ring. In addition to the *tallit*, the bride often gave the groom gold or silver chains, a Haggadah for Passover and a beautiful watch. This custom of gift giving continues in many communities to the present time.

Today the dress at Jewish weddings varies with the wishes of the couple. A majority of brides still wear white gowns, whether purchased at a store or handmade. In some instances, the bride is married in a dress worn by her grandmother or mother, symbolic of family continuity. Other brides opt for less formal attire, preferring to be married in a simpler dress selected for the occasion. The color of the dress is not important, and increasing numbers of brides have moved away from the formality of a white gown to dresses more reflective of their individual taste. No bride, therefore, should ever feel less "authentic" in the dress she will always treasure as "my wedding gown."

Finally, there is the old adage that the bride should wear "something old, something new, something borrowed and something blue." While some Jewish brides follow this prescription, it has no basis in Jewish tradition and is, rather. a custom borrowed from the larger culture.

Grooms may wear tuxedos, suits or even more casual clothing. The choice is yours.

THERE ARE THOSE WHO SAY

Love was the last gift that God created. Very late in the sixth day, God realized that Adam was incomplete. He was missing part of his soul. So, God created Eve. All of the angels gathered to witness the marriage. The sun began to set and God painted the sky with streaks of red and violet and orange. The birds brought branches of dogwood and cedar for the *chupah*. The scent of myrrh was in the air, and the most gentle breeze kissed the faces of the bride and groom.

God officiated. As a wedding gift, God gave two letters of his own name to Adam and to Eve. To Adam God gave a *yud* and to Eve a *hey*. So, Adam was called *ish* and Eve was called *ishah*.

So, I believe, marriage is called *kiddushin*, holiness, because a husband and wife each brings a different aspect of God to their union. It is an act of completion and wholeness. It is an act in which God participates as a partner. It is a holy act.

Rabbi Steven M. Rosman

PICTURES OF US ON OUR
WEDDING DAY

THE GROOM

THE BRIDE

PHOTO

PHOTO

Record the special significance of any item of clothing you wore:

_____

_____

_____

_____

_____

_____

_____

_____

_____

The Wedding Ring

One of the ways in which the Talmud states that Jews can become betrothed is by exchanging an object of value, usually a coin worth at least a *perutah* (roughly a penny). Over time, some say, this practice evolved into the custom of the groom giving his bride a ring. Today, of course, double-ring ceremonies are quite common in Reform and Conservative ceremonies.

According to Orthodox Jewish law, the groom is responsible for obtaining the ring. It may be a family heirloom or new, but it has to be the groom's property, inasmuch as he is giving it as a gift to the bride. Accordingly, the ring cannot be borrowed.

Some say that Jewish history is a chain of interlocking rings, and therefore that the wedding ring symbolizes both our link to the past and our commitment to the future. Others view the ring as a circle, whole, unbroken, having no beginning and no end. Similarly, they say, love never ends.

The Bible reflects a view of rings as a repository of power for good or evil. Pharaoh gave Joseph his ring, and Joseph used its authority to save Egypt. In like fashion, a husband and wife confer a certain power upon one another by exchanging rings, a power that must be used wisely, lest it damage the relationship.

Traditionally, the rabbis insisted that the wedding ring be a metal band, lest there be any suspicion that the bride was marrying for the sake of a gift or lest the poor be embarrassed by their inability to compete with the rings of the wealthy. The ring was also to be without precious stones so that the bride could not be misled as to its value. In some European communities a few centuries ago, couples used a large, magnificently crafted, communally owned marriage ring for their ceremony, replacing it thereafter with their own.

A ring is not required for a Jewish wedding. To this day, some Sephardic Jews use a coin rather than a ring. In addition, more than one couple has used an actual coin from antiquity as part of the wedding service in addition to the rings. This is a beautiful possibility, one that symbolically binds us to our ancestors.

HOW WE SELECTED OUR
WEDDING RINGS

The Guest List

Beginning in talmudic times, the rabbis required at least a *minyan*, ten male Jews, at every wedding, two of whom served as witnesses. Orthodox and many Conservative Jews maintain that practice today. Within more liberal Conservative circles and in all of Reform Judaism, such a *minyan* is desirable but not mandatory. Reform Judaism and segments of Conservative Judaism count women and men equally as members of the *minyan* and as witnesses.

The custom of limiting wedding invitations to a selected group is a relatively modern development in Judaism. In eighteenth- and nineteenth-century Eastern Europe, most weddings involved the entire community. By sharing in a *simcha*, each man and woman present fulfilled the *mitzvah* of rejoicing with the bride and groom. Recently, this Eastern European custom was reflected in the presence of 5000 guests at the wedding of the granddaughter of a prominent Brooklyn Hasidic rabbi.

The great medieval Jewish teacher Rabbi Eliezer ben Isaac went so far as to compare wedding guests to the Israelites of old who stood at the foot of Mount Sinai to receive the Torah. For he saw in the joining of a couple in marriage a glimpse of the sacred, a manifestation of God's presence in the physical world.

In the State of Israel, we often see Jewish history re-created on kibbutzim, where all kibbutz members join in marking this happy occasion. In North America, however, in the absence of a close-knit, proximate "village" of Jews, personal invitations have become the rule rather than the exception.

The guest list at contemporary Jewish weddings reflects the wishes of the bride, the groom and their families. One of the most difficult decisions in most wedding preparations, it requires families to determine who is most important to them. Obviously, parents, grandparents, siblings and their families should be present. Beyond the immediate family, the wedding guests should consist ideally of those men, women and children who have been— and will continue to be—part of your life. You are asking them to share a moment in which two families bond together as one, joined by your love for one another.

THOSE WHO SHARED
OUR WEDDING DAY

—————————————————————   —————————————————————

—————————————————————   —————————————————————

—————————————————————   —————————————————————

—————————————————————   —————————————————————

—————————————————————   —————————————————————

—————————————————————   —————————————————————

—————————————————————   —————————————————————

—————————————————————   —————————————————————

—————————————————————   —————————————————————

—————————————————————   —————————————————————

—————————————————————   —————————————————————

—————————————————————   —————————————————————

—————————————————————   —————————————————————

—————————————————————   —————————————————————

—————————————————————   —————————————————————

—————————————————————   —————————————————————

THOSE WHO SHARED
OUR WEDDING DAY

The Rabbi and the Cantor

Many Jews are unaware that Jewish law, *halachah*, does not require a rabbi to perform a wedding. An observant male Jew, knowledgeable in the Jewish wedding and divorce rituals, may officiate in the presence of two Shabbat-observing adult male witnesses. Still, it has become virtually universal practice for a rabbi and/or cantor to solemnize the marriage.

Jewish midrashic literature portrays God as having personally officiated at the marriage of Adam and Eve, with the angels of heaven present as the wedding guests, then dancing and playing music for the world's first couple in ten bridal chambers prepared and furnished by God.

The choice of a rabbi for the wedding is a decision that should be made by the bride and groom together. Most couples ask a rabbi whom they both know and respect to officiate—the rabbi from their childhood synagogue, for example, a relative or a rabbi they have come to know as adults.

Many couples desire that more than one rabbi participate. So long as each rabbi is comfortable sharing the ceremony that you envision, their presence can significantly enhance the beauty of your wedding day.

The same is true for cantors. A wedding's music can create a sense of the sacred. The participation of a cantor who has been close to one or both of you adds a special dimension.

If you do not have your own rabbi or cantor, speak to friends and ask for their suggestions. Whether you have known the rabbi or cantor for many years or have just met, however, you should make an appointment to discuss the ceremony several months in advance. If you have special requests for music or the ritual, feel free to express them. More often than not, the right rabbi or cantor will try to make your wedding day uniquely yours.

THOSE WHO BLESSED US
ON OUR WEDDING DAY

_____   _____
Name   Name

How we found them: _____

_____

_____

_____

_____

_____

Special moments with them: _____

_____

_____

_____

_____

_____

_____

_____

_____

_____

_____

THERE ARE THOSE
WHO SAY

There are those who say

Three things bring great satisfaction:
a beautiful home, a beautiful wife,
and beautiful clothes.   *Talmud*

Every bride is beautiful and graceful.
                                Talmud

The
Wedding Day
Approaches

The Aufruf

Aufruf (pronounced "owf-roof" or, more colloquially "oof-roof") is a German word meaning "calling up" and refers to a synagogue celebration on the Shabbat preceding the wedding. According to the rabbis, King Solomon built a gate in the Jerusalem Temple where Jews would sit on Shabbat and honor new grooms. When the Temple was destroyed in 70 C.E. and the institution of the synagogue gained strength, a form of the ancient Solomonic practice moved into the synagogue. Eventually, this custom became known as the *aufruf*.

The *aufruf* is a colorful rite in many synagogues. On the Shabbat morning prior to the wedding, the prospective groom—and in many synagogues the prospective bride as well—are called to the Torah for an *aliyah* (the honor of reciting or chanting the blessings before and after the reading of a section of the Torah). In addition to the *aliyah*, some couples study and prepare a short talk. This may be an interpretation of the *sedra*, the weekly Shabbat Torah reading, or thoughts on another Jewish theme that holds special meaning for them as they near their wedding day.

The rabbi then usually says a few words of congratulations on behalf of the congregation and may also present a gift from the synagogue, usually a Jewish book or ritual object for the couple's new home. This segment of the service concludes with a blessing for the couple's happiness.

Just before the bride- and groom-to-be leave the *bimah* (pulpit), the congregation sometimes showers them with raisins, nuts and candy, indicative of their good wishes for a sweet and fulfilling marriage. Children attending the service wait until the coast is clear, race to the front of the sanctuary, gather up as much loose candy as they can and then return to their seats for the rest of the service.

In times past, the rabbis invested the prospective groom's being showered with raisins and nuts, usually almonds, with great symbolic significance. They indicated that, just as almonds and raisins may be either sweet or bitter, so a marriage may be either sweet or bitter, depending upon the character of those who are a part of it.

In many Reform and Conservative congregations today, the spirit of the *aufruf* is preserved through a blessing by the rabbi, without the *aliyah* or showering with candy and nuts.

Wedding Week Parties

North American bridal showers and prewedding bachelor parties have become fairly common in the Jewish community, though ostentation is frowned upon and good taste encouraged. These afternoon or evening gatherings literally shower the future bride and groom with the expressed affection of close personal and family friends, as well as practical or gag gifts for their home. More often than not, these wedding parties also afford an opportunity for reminiscences of younger days and good times, when lifelong bonds of friendship took root. In truth, though they have taken on very different forms, bridal showers and bachelor parties are not new to Judaism.

In nineteenth-century Eastern Europe, for example, friends of the groom often paraded through the village streets, their friend atop their shoulders, bound for the synagogue and an evening of tribute in story and song. To this day, Sephardic men host soon-to-be-married friends in male-only evening celebrations of food, drink and a "roast."

Until recently, women's parties tended to be much more subdued than those of men. The Sephardic community in particular, even today, preserves customs developed over many centuries. During the week prior to the wedding, the bride's female family and friends gather for an afternoon or evening of food and song. The melodies are usually romantic, the humor gentle. In some Middle Eastern Jewish communities, the bride's mother feeds her seven times, the mystical number 7 symbolizing good luck and good fortune. In other lands, the bride's hands and feet are daubed with a reddish mixture containing henna, a custom borne of the superstitious belief that this ritual will protect her from evil spirits.

Gift giving was—and is—common at these gatherings. Depending upon the wishes of the couple and the party's host, presents range from the simple to the extravagant. More and more frequently, specifically Jewish gifts have become presents of choice: a Chanukah menorah, a Passover seder plate, a mezuzah, or a Shabbat Havdalah set. But more important than the actual object is the spirit in which it is given, with heartfelt warm wishes for a married life of love and fulfillment.

FRIENDS WHO GATHERED
AT PARTIES TO WISH US WELL

Bride

_____   _____

_____   _____

_____   _____

_____   _____

_____   _____

_____   _____

_____   _____

Groom

_____   _____

_____   _____

_____   _____

_____   _____

_____   _____

_____   _____

_____   _____

THERE ARE THOSE WHO SAY

Hospitality is greater than welcoming God's presence. The hospitable person is rewarded both in this world and in the world to come. *Talmud*

Laughter is a universal bond that draws all people closer together. *Jewish Folk Saying*

There is no joy like the joy of the heart. *Ben Sirach*

The joy of the heart begets song. *Zohar*

Visiting the Mikveh

Virtually all Orthodox, many Conservative and some Reform and Reconstructionist brides visit the *mikveh*, the Jewish ritual bath, prior to the wedding. While most *mikvaot* are indoor community institutions, any body of *mayim chayim*, running or "living" water, qualifies as acceptable. Especially in areas with a warm climate, the natural setting of an ocean, lake or river may be preferred.

Visiting the *mikveh* can be a powerful spiritual Jewish religious experience. Indeed, countless men and women who have converted to Judaism cite the instant of emerging from the *mikveh*'s waters as the moment when they truly became Jews. By the same token, Orthodox Jewish tradition considers the *mikveh* ritual a symbolic act of rebirth for women about to be married, when they immerse themselves in water, which in rabbinic eyes originated with the world's creation in the Garden of Eden. As such, holds mystical Jewish lore, they are reborn and come to their wedding ceremony in innocence and purity.

If you are among those who visited the *mikveh* before your wedding, the experience is undoubtedly one you will long remember. Your rabbi can review the ritual of *mikveh* with you and guide you to the *mikveh* closest to your home.

A Letter to Parents

The night prior to your wedding is most often a time of reflection and deep emotion, a period when you call to mind the course of your life and the love and caring of the many people who have brought you to this day.

If you wish to give your parents a gift that they will treasure more than any material object, use these hours to write them a letter in which you share what is in your heart. Though not a custom in Judaism, this testimony of love and gratitude will assuredly have a treasured place in your parents' home throughout their lives.

In your letter, you may choose to recall moments from childhood or young adulthood when the bond between you was felt most strongly, when you recognized the sacrifices they made on your behalf, when you felt most secure and safe in their embrace.

Whether you present this letter to them at the wedding or mail it so that it arrived a few days later, be assured that it will be read and reread as a touching tribute from child to parent with a meaning beyond measure.

THERE ARE THOSE WHO SAY

Dear Dad,

It hardly seems possible that tomorrow is my wedding day and that you won't be there. When I was a little girl and pretended to be a bride, I always imagined that you would walk me down the aisle. Even though you are physically gone, I believe totally that you are in heaven looking down and wondering how I am. So I'm writing this letter to you so that you won't worry about me.

Steven is wonderful, Dad. I'm deeply in love with him, and I like him too! In many ways, he's just like you. Steven is kind and generous and affectionate. Oh, he has a temper, but he says what's on his mind and then lets it go. Just like you used to do.

He cares about people and wants to help them. His friends tell me that he is going to be a great doctor. Just like you.

He tells me to aim for the stars—and he means it. He values my work as much as his practice, and even when he is exhausted, he makes time for us to talk and be together.

You'll be happy to know that we've already joined the synagogue. The rabbi is terrific, and we plan to get involved. No children for at least a year or two, but they will grow up in a Jewish home and will know you through all the stories I will tell them about their Grandpa Mike.

I miss you terribly, Dad. Tomorrow, when I walk down the aisle, I will feel your spirit beside me. And in my heart of hearts, I know that you will be there, somewhere, whispering "You did good, Patty. You did good."

I love you!
Patty

THERE ARE THOSE WHO SAY

Dear Mom and Dad,

It's 2:00 in the morning and I can't sleep. In less than twenty-four hours I will be a married man, and the enormity of that commitment just won't let me drift off. I don't have a single doubt as to my love for Linda or as to the rightness of our joining our lives together. When all is said and done, my emotions are most likely due to the realization that I will now have a new home, one that Linda and I will have to create together.

I want to thank you for giving me a model for the kind of home I want for my family, and for the countless ways in which you helped me grow to adulthood.

Thank you for all the nights you let me come into your bed when I had nightmares.

Thank you for all the nights you sat at my bedside when I was sick.

Thank you for all the hours you spent helping me with homework I couldn't understand—especially geometry!

Thank you for making sure that I had new clothes to wear to school, even when buying them meant that you couldn't get things for yourselves.

Thank you for letting me know that you loved me every day of my life, for all your hugs and kisses, and reassuring silent gestures that required no words.

Thank you for making me go to religious school and Shabbat services, even when I didn't want to, for celebrating the Jewish holidays in our home, and for being such proud Jews yourselves.

Thank you for being on my side, even when I was wrong and you told me so.

Thank you for believing in me and for teaching me to believe in myself.

I don't know what the future will bring. I do know, though, that I am ready for whatever life brings, with Linda as my wife, lover, partner and friend.

Thank you for giving me life, for giving me love, for teaching me what it means to care for another human being. I love you with all my heart, and am proud to be your son.

Love,

Jerry

THE BRIDE:
A LETTER TO MY PARENTS

_____

_____

_____

_____

_____

_____

_____

_____

_____

_____

_____

_____

_____

_____

_____

_____

_____

_____

_____

_____

_____

THE GROOM:
A LETTER TO MY PARENTS

_____

_____

_____

_____

_____

_____

_____

_____

_____

_____

_____

_____

_____

_____

_____

_____

_____

_____

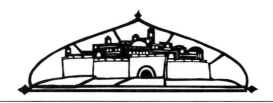

THE RABBIS SAY

You are probably nervous—and you have every right to be. You are about to take the most important step of your life. This is forever. Yes, even marriages that end in divorce are forever. You don't share a home, a bed, a child, a legal entity, a washing machine—all that marriage entails—without indelibility. It's a big step.

But I don't mean to make it sound grim. Marriage is also delightful—and fun. It is exciting to continue to make discoveries about another person, with whom one is already in love, and to venture together into areas and activities that didn't seem appropriate for a single person. It is delightful and fun as long as you avoid a few things. All you need do is "avoid." Some people say, "You have to work at marriage." That sounds so laborious. There's enough work at work. All you have to do is avoid a few simple and rather thoughtless things.

Like expecting perfection (which usually means "the way I think it ought to be").

Like imagining that when your spouse is cross or grumpy, you are the target, either the innocent or the guilty object, when the reason is entirely something external to the marriage and totally unrelated to you.

You can also avoid "in-law-itis," which is

almost always well intentioned but which requires deep understanding and a judicious, well-timed mixture of patience and independence.

One more thing to avoid is being more a taker than a giver. If there has to be any competition between you, let it be who can give more to the other.

A rabbi is also expected to urge you to have a richly observant Jewish home, to do the whole "shabbat thing"—the candles, the wine, the challah, the guests. To attend synagogue regularly, to put up a *sukah* or, if you can't have one, to eat at least one meal in one or say the prayers in one, and many more home rituals. We don't say these things only because we are expected to do so. We know that where there is such observance, such self-discipline, such a context, a value is put on values; that in such a home, there will be no "anything goes" attitude; that in such a home, the children will know that they are Jewish and will enjoy being Jewish. And where those observances have begun with the marriage, your children will know that they have been born into Judaism, that it is real, that it is authentic. When they sense that, Judaism will become part of them and they will become part of it. It will be good for you and good for your marriage, and will give you an extra sense of substance in knowing that millions of Jews throughout the world are performing in concert, albeit physically invisible to each other. I wish you well.

Rabbi Joseph B. Glaser

You are about to enter into the most important agreement you have ever or will ever make in your lifetime. If you've each made the right choice, and I assume and pray that you have, you are embarking on a trip to ecstasy, "Gan Eden."

There is nothing better than coming home to someone who is eagerly awaiting your arrival. There is no greater feeling than being wanted and needed. The sparks of love you will generate each evening after being apart all day will make your apartment into a castle, your home into a palace. Will it happen that way? You bet it will—if you want it. What stands in the way?

Happiness is not something you can buy or acquire. It is only something you can give. You are madly in love right now. By definition, this means that you each want to be the prime source of joy in each other's lives. So, do it. Each day ask yourselves, what can I do today to improve my spouse's joy in life? Is there anything I can do tomorrow that will be better than what I did today? When two people spend years attempting to outdo one another in an effort to improve the other's life, they are approaching ecstasy.

One caution: Ecstasy is not found in things. It's found in a soft touch, a kind look, a gentle word and a patient smile.

When you have love in your heart, your voice is soft and inviting, your eyes reflect desire, the touch of your hands is reassuring and you make one another feel secure.

Happiness is really a state of reaching your goals. Is it too much to ask that, from this day forward, your goal should be to add joy to the life of the other? Strive for it. It's worth every effort, and if you achieve your goal, the reward will be happiness. All the best in your endeavor.

Rabbi Joseph H. Ehrenkranz

The Wedding Day Begins

The Morning of the Wedding Day

Fasting

In times past, the future bride and groom traditionally awoke in their respective parents' homes and began a fast that ended only during the ceremony, when they shared the wine under the *chupah*, and subsequently at their party.

Jewish tradition teaches that all past sins are forgiven on a wedding day. Therefore, the day gradually acquired the characteristics of a quasi-Yom Kippur. Not only did the future bride and groom refrain from food and drink, but they also recited the *viddui* (confession of Yom Kippur in the afternoon service). Customarily, the wedding took place in the late afternoon, so as to enable as complete a fast as possible.

The rabbis of the Talmud saw the fast as a sign of contrition and, just as important, as a guarantee of sobriety. They also perceived the fast as a reenactment of the drama of Sinai, where Israel, by accepting the Torah, consummated a "marriage" with God. Just as the Israelites prepared for their betrothal, said the rabbis, so it is fitting that a bride and groom do likewise. The custom of fasting is preserved by many Orthodox and Conservative couples today.

In Yemenite homes even today, many grooms go to their mothers on their wedding day, asking forgiveness for any hurt they may have caused them in the past. The son kneels and kisses her knees, after which his mother gives him a coin to be used as a ring substitute in the wedding service.

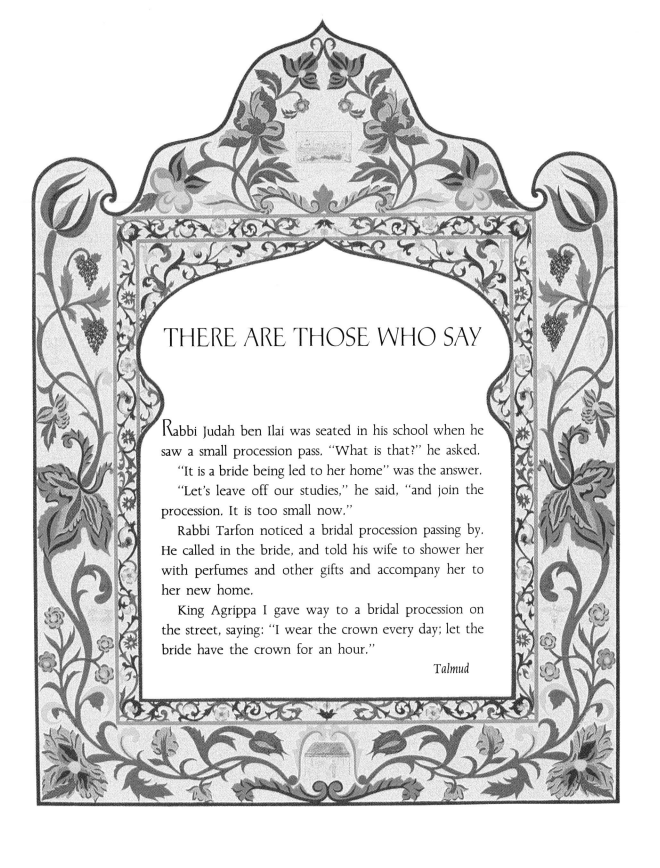

THERE ARE THOSE WHO SAY

Rabbi Judah ben Ilai was seated in his school when he saw a small procession pass. "What is that?" he asked.

"It is a bride being led to her home" was the answer.

"Let's leave off our studies," he said, "and join the procession. It is too small now."

Rabbi Tarfon noticed a bridal procession passing by. He called in the bride, and told his wife to shower her with perfumes and other gifts and accompany her to her new home.

King Agrippa I gave way to a bridal procession on the street, saying: "I wear the crown every day; let the bride have the crown for an hour."

Talmud

OUR EMOTIONS AS WE AWOKE
ON OUR WEDDING DAY

Bride

_____

_____

_____

_____

_____

_____

_____

_____

Groom

_____

_____

_____

_____

_____

_____

_____

_____

Coming to the Ceremony

In the Orthodox communities of Eastern Europe, the groom came to the courtyard of the synagogue accompanied by his family, the rabbi and his friends. Musicians, called *klezmorim*, usually playing a violin, bass and clarinet, led the way, sometimes in a torchlight procession. Shortly thereafter, the *klezmorim* departed, met the bride and led her and her family to the courtyard. There she and her groom were showered with barley and all the guests cried out, *"Peru urevu"* ("Be fruitful and multiply") three times.

In recent years there has been a resurgence of interest in *klezmer*, and today there are a number of *klezmer* bands made up of young Jewish musicians who seek to preserve the rich *klezmer* heritage. The old phrase "wedding without *klezmorim*" connoted a dull event. The melodies of the *klezmer* genre can be electric in their impact, bringing groups of Jews to their feet in an almost innate reaction to the uniquely Jewish music of days gone by.

Traditionally, barley was a symbol of fertility, and throwing it on the young couple was an expression of the community's hope that the couple would have many children. A number of scholars believe that the Christian custom of throwing rice at a bride and groom as they leave the church grew directly out of this Jewish practice.

"Peru urevu" is the first of the Torah's 613 commandments. As such, say the rabbis, it highlights Judaism's esteem for a family with children and, thus, is most appropriate as a good wish for the beginning of the wedding.

Today, when Jews no longer live in small villages, the distances to be traveled between home and ceremony have all but eliminated the processional. Elements of it, however, are preserved in the wedding processional itself and at the party following the ceremony.

The Ketubah

In times past, upon arriving at the place where the wedding was to be held, the bride and groom went into separate rooms. At the *chossen's tish*, the Yiddish term for "groom's table," the groom affirmed his willingness to accept the obligations spelled out in the Ketubah, the Jewish wedding contract.

Ketubah literally means "written," and refers to the marriage contract signed and read at Jewish weddings.

Most scholars assert that the *ketubah* first emerged during the Babylonian exile, following the destruction of the Temple in 586 B.C.E. The Talmud, however, states that King David gave a *ketubah* to his wives, and the Jewish scholar Maimonides also assigns it an earlier date. Whenever it first came into use, the present-day Orthodox text was fixed about 200 B.C.E. and was composed in Aramaic, the Jewish community's most common language at that time.

Every bride received as her property from her groom a *ketubah*, a legal document that protected her rights. The contract specified the groom's financial obligations, including a minimum divorce settlement and a minimum inheritance in case of the husband's death. In addition, the *ketubah* specified the Torah-based woman's right to food, clothing and conjugal rights, as well as the husband's responsibility to "care for her, provide for her and cherish her." The Talmud elaborates on these basic Torah

stipulations. Indeed, two talmudic tractates, *kiddushin* and *ketubot*, deal with marriage laws. Among other things, the laws state that a husband must:

- Give his wife a *ketubah*.
- Ransom her if she is kidnapped.
- Support her out of his estate (in the case of divorce).
- Support any daughters out of his estate until they are married.

Sexual fidelity was the right and responsibility of both partners. The wife had to go with her husband wherever he asked her to live, with two exceptions. She could demand that they establish a home in the land of Israel and, once there, demand that they live in Jerusalem.

The ancient *ketubah* represented a major step forward in women's rights. In a world in which women were often viewed as chattel, Judaism affirmed that every bride was to be accorded dignity and security in the marriage relationship.

The *ketubah* originally was one of the great artistic breakthroughs of Jewish tradition. Usually on parchment, written by hand, and often illuminated in brilliant color, it manifested an artistic expression often stifled because of Judaism's prohibition against creating graven images.

Over the centuries, every country in which Jews lived had *ketubot*, often containing symbols

and objects that characterized that nation's unique folk art. In Persia, for example, the *ketubah* frequently included the lion of Judah, the rising sun of the Persian empire and ornate oriental carpets. North African *ketubot* had many geometric shapes, while Italian ones almost always portrayed cherubs, birds and flowers. By the same token, the *ketubot* of Jews living in poverty or in lands of oppression were often written on plain, simple paper. In reality, these *ketubot*, especially those written in the displaced persons' camps following the Holocaust, are as beautiful in their symbolic message of hope and confidence in a better future as any commissioned document.

Since, unlike the Torah, there is no rigidly fixed format for a *ketubah*, artists were not limited to parchment or to special pens or ink. Magnificent paper-cut *ketubot* were created, and, in time, printed *ketubot* such as those often seen today. The art of the *ketubah*, then, fulfilled the principle of *hiddur mitzvah*, "adornment of a *mitzvah*." Today, centuries later, we still view the work of our forebears with admiration and awe.

Modern *ketubot*, like wedding invitations, take advantage of high-quality, high-speed printing techniques. Dozens of beautiful *ketubot*, some reproductions of original art, are readily available. There has also been a resurgence in the use of handmade *ketubot*. Fine Jewish artisans throughout the world have begun to devote their talent to the creation of stunning marriage contracts.

More significant than the change in artistic style, however, has been the change in substance of the *ketubah*. Sensitive to the male-oriented language of the ancient document and contemporary values, many modern texts have been equalized. That is, both bride and groom make the same commitments to each other.

In ancient times, as today, the *ketubah* was signed just prior to the wedding ceremony. Prepared far enough in advance to be ready for the wedding, it required two male witnesses unrelated to each other, the bride or the groom. Today, especially in Reform Judaism, both men and women are honored by being asked to certify the beginning of a new couple's life together. In addition, the bride and groom themselves often sign the document.

A PHOTOGRAPH OF
OUR KETUBAH

KETUBOT—OLD AND NEW

1. United States, 1979.
2. Iran, early 20th century.
3. Displaced person's camp, Germany, 1947.
4. United States, 1990.

בזמילה עשר ימים ללודש כסלו
שנת ושמשה אלפים ושבע מאות ועשרים
ושמנה לבריאת העולם למנין שאנו מנין כאן במדינה
ברוקלין שבמדינת אמעריקא הבפנית איך הוחן אליהו בר
ר ישראל הכהנה ואמר לה להדא בתולתא ביכא ווזי
בת ר אברהם יצחק המכונה סענסר הוי לי לאנתו כדת מיעד
וישראל ואנא אפלוז ואוקיר ואיזון ואפרנס יתכי ליכי כהלכות גבריי
יהודאין דפלהין ומוקירין וזנין ומפרנסין לנשיהון בקושטא והיבנא
בתולכי כסף זוזי מאתן דחזי ליכי מדאוריתא ומזוניכי וסיפוקיכי
ומיעל לותיכי כאורה כל ארעא וצביאת מרת ביכא ווזה בתולתא דא והותלה
למאנתו ודן נדוניא דהנעלת לה מבי אבוה בין בכסף בין בדהב בין בתכשיטין
במאני דלבושא בשימושי דירה ובשימושי דערסא הכל קבל עליו ר אליהו חתן
דן במאה זקוקים כסף צריף וצבי ר אליהו וחתן דן והוסיף לה מן דיליה עוד מאה
זקוקים כסף צריף אחרים בנדד סך הכל מאתים זקוקים כסף צריף וכך אמר
ר אליהו חתן דן אחריות שטר כתובתא דא נדוניא דן ותוספתא דא קבלית
עלי ועל ירתי בתראי להתפרע מכל שפר ארג נכסין וקנינין דאית לי דרעורת כל
שמיא דקנאי ודעתיד אנא למקנא נכסין דאית להון אחריות ודלית להון
אחריות כלהון יהון אחראין וערבאין לפרוע מנהון שטר כתובתא דא נדוניא
דן ותוספתא דא מנאי ואפילו מן גלימא דעל כתפאי בחיי ובתר חיי
ותוספתא דא קבל עליו ר אליהו חתן דן בחומר כל שטר כתובות
ותוספתא דנהגין בבנות ישראל העשוין כתקן וכתיקון חכמים זכרונם
לברכה דלא כאסמכתא ודלא כטופסי דשטרי וקנינא
מן ר אליהו בר ר ישראל וחתן דן
למרת ביכא ווזה בת ר אברהם יצחק בתולתא
דא על כל מה דכתוב ומפורש לעיל במנא
דכשר לקנויא ביה והכל
שריר וקים

5.

6.

7.

8.

Veiling the Bride

In Eastern Europe of old, and in many traditional Jewish settings today, the customs of *bazetzen di kalah*, "seating the bride," and *badeken di kalah*, "veiling the bride," take place immediately after the *ketubah* is signed.

In centuries past, the bride was seated on a beautiful thronelike chair, with her women friends around her, offering blessings and singing songs. The chair was often covered with a white sheet and flowers. The bride's hair was cut off, then replaced with a *sheitl*, or wig. Afterwards, a singer called the *badchan* (jester) serenaded the bride with gloomy songs, allowing all persons present to give full expression to their feelings of nostalgia and sadness over the remarkable speed with which a child becomes an adult.

The Jews of Eastern Europe saw a woman's hair as a potentially powerful sexual temptation to men. Accordingly, a woman's locks were shorn and replaced with a wig, presumably to decrease her sexual appeal. While some chasidic Jews still follow this practice, it has been all but totally eliminated in most branches of Judaism. *Bazetzen di kalah* itself, however, is still a fixture at virtually all Orthodox and many Conservative Jewish weddings.

Badeken di kalah was the next formalized step on the path to the *chupah*. The groom entered and looked at the bride. Then he covered her face with the veil while the biblical blessing over the matriarch Rebekah was recited: "Our sister, may you be the mother of...tens of thousands" (Genesis 24:60). The groom then departed, after which the bride's friends danced around her, gently showering her with raisins and nuts.

As we noted previously, the practice of wearing a veil derives from the account in Genesis 24:65 of how Rebekah covered her face with a veil when she saw her husband-to-be, Isaac, approaching. Over the centuries, other commentators saw the veil as a protection from the "evil eye," as a safeguard against lustful leering by other men, and even as a means of insuring that the groom would not notice a pimple or scar on the bride's face and call off the wedding!

One beautiful interpretation asserts that, just as one often covers one's eyes during the *shema* as an expression of concentration upon and trust in God, so does a bride cover her eyes as a symbol of trust in her husband.

The widespread custom of the groom's not seeing the bride in her gown prior to the wedding is not a Jewish practice. Ever since our ancestor Jacob was tricked into marrying Leah rather than Rachel, Jewish grooms have assured themselves before the ceremony that the woman they were to marry was in fact their intended. Avoidance of seeing one another before the wedding is a borrowed custom, based on the superstition that it will somehow bring bad luck.

In more liberal branches of Judaism, the mother, grandmother or sisters of the bride frequently fix and lower the veil, with tears of sadness and joy, with a kiss and often with a blessing as well.

HOW I FELT AS
MY WEDDING VEIL WAS LOWERED

THERE ARE THOSE WHO SAY

When the heart is full, the eyes overflow. *Sholom Aleichem*

How like a lovely flower, so fair, so pure thou art;
I watch thee and a prayer comes stealing through my heart;
I lay my hands upon thee and ask God to adjure
That thou shalt be forever so sweet, so fair, so pure. *Heinrich Heine*

The Wedding Ceremony

The Procession

In the traditional weddings in Eastern Europe, immediately after *badeken di kalah*, the wedding procession began. First, the *klezmorim* led the groom to the *chupah*, accompanied by his parents or by his father and father-in-law. They then returned for the bride and her parents, or her mother and mother-in-law. These escorts, in Hebrew *shoshvinim*, symbolically reenacted part of the wedding of the first couple, Adam and Eve.

The Shoshvinim

According to the rabbis, the angels Michael and Gabriel escorted Adam to his marriage to Eve. Out of this legend evolved the custom of *shoshvinim*, or, in Yiddish, *unterfuhrers*, which was formalized in talmudic times.

These escorts often carried candles. In Judaism, the marriage of a man and woman is likened to the joining of God and Israel at Mount Sinai. The Book of Exodus states that on the day the Torah was given, "there was thunder and lightning" (i.e., lights). Just as there were lights at the bonding of God and Israel, so there are often candles at a Jewish wedding.

As the centuries passed, the order of the wedding procession slowly changed. At first, friends joined parents in the entourage, gradually taking on the roles of best man and maid/matron of honor.

In North America today, there may be a number of men and women friends in the wedding party. In addition, especially in second marriages, children of the bride and groom often stand under the *chupah* and may even have a role in the ceremony itself. Though far from universal, a number of communities preserve the ancient custom of escorts leading the way and carrying lighted candles. Since there is no strictly prescribed order for the procession, it may be as short—or long—as you choose to make it.

The wedding procession with which modern Jews are most familiar begins with the entrance of the groom, either alone or accompanied by his parents. Some interpreters state that, just as God waited at Sinai for God's bride (Israel), so does the groom wait for his bride to appear.

The grandparents of the couple enter, then the best man and maid/matron of honor, the groom's parents, and finally the mother of the bride, usually accompanied by a son, grandchild or other family member or friend.

There is a pause, the music changes, and at last the bride appears. Yemenite brides are sometimes preceded by a group of singing women. Most frequently, the father of the bride escorts his daughter down the aisle. The groom walks to the father, shakes his hand, takes his bride's arm and leads her to the *chupah*. This practice may have its origin in the way

some primitive societies arranged marriages. A father would lead his daughter between two lines of unmarried tribal males. Whoever reached out and "claimed" her had thus selected a wife. A father's escorting, then, is a borrowed rather than a uniquely Jewish custom. Increasingly today, both parents escort the bride down the aisle.

Together, the couple then comes to the *chupah*, with the bride to the right of the groom. The Book of Psalms reads: "The queen stands on your right hand in gold of Ophir." Since a Jewish bride on her wedding day is seen as a queen, she stands on the groom's right.

Music

It is most appropriate to use Jewish music in Jewish wedding ceremonies during the procession to the *chupah* and the ceremony's conclusion. Increasingly, Jewish couples have moved away from the melodies of secular composers, such as Wagner, to Israeli, chasidic or North American Jewish compositions. The rabbi, cantor, friends or family may have suggestions you deem right for you. Secure a tape of the songs, listen to them and then decide.

OUR WEDDING PROCESSION

The Order

_____

_____

_____

_____

_____

_____

_____

_____

_____

_____

_____

_____

_____

_____

_____

_____

_____

_____

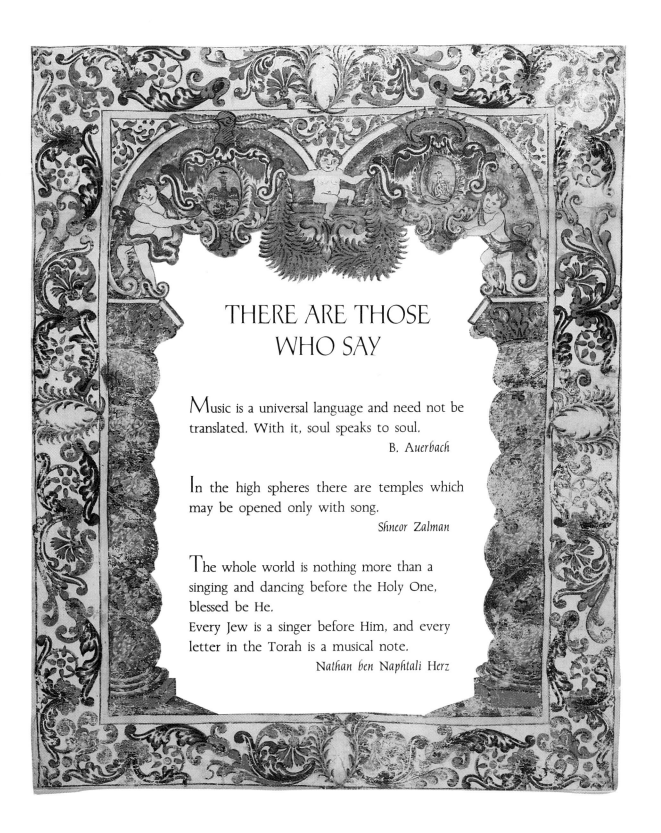

THERE ARE THOSE
WHO SAY

Music is a universal language and need not be translated. With it, soul speaks to soul.

B. Auerbach

In the high spheres there are temples which may be opened only with song.

Shneor Zalman

The whole world is nothing more than a singing and dancing before the Holy One, blessed be He.

Every Jew is a singer before Him, and every letter in the Torah is a musical note.

Nathan ben Naphtali Herz

MUSIC AT OUR WEDDING

During the procession:

Name of piece   Composer

_____

_____

_____

_____

_____

_____

During the ceremony

_____

_____

_____

_____

_____

At the conclusion of the ceremony

_____

_____

_____

_____

The Chupah

The *chupah* or marriage canopy, is a ritualization of the ancient rite of *nissuin*. *Nissuin* originally consisted of the wife being escorted to her husband's house to consummate the marriage. Over time, the *chupah* came to refer to a special room where the couple retired after the wedding service for a period of seclusion, known as *yichud*.

By the Middle Ages, the *chupah* had evolved into a canopy symbolizing the home, and a reminder as well of the humble homes of our nomadic biblical ancestors. This canopy was supported by four poles, under which the bride, groom and family stood during the wedding.

Beginning in ancient times, when a boy was born, a cedar tree was planted. At the birth of a girl, an acacia tree was planted. When the children grew up and were to be married, the poles with which to support their *chupah* were made from those very trees. Today, especially in Israel, where cedar and acacia trees are plentiful, this ancient custom is preserved.

However, such elaborate preparations were not required. The *chupah* often was, and is, a plain *tallit* or velvet cloth supported by four poles held by friends. In addition, the groom's *tallit* was, and is, sometimes drawn over the heads of both him and his bride, especially if the bride has given it to him as a gift. In France, the groom covered the bride's head with his *tallit* as a symbol of sheltering her. In Sephardic ceremonies today, grooms sometimes wrap themselves and their brides with a *tallit* during the ceremony. Modern Jews may use a *tallit*, a free-standing canopy or some other portable *chupah* provided by the rabbi or synagogue.

If you choose a *chupah* with poles held by family members or friends, you can be certain that being asked to perform this role is an honor they will long remember. Nephews, nieces—or, in second marriages, children—never forget their opportunity to participate in helping to sanctify a Jewish moment in time.

THE RABBIS SAY

There is a Hebrew phrase, *Laamod dom*, which means "to stand in silence" or "to stand at attention." That phrase defines my attitude toward you who are on the verge of a life together. I stand in awe of the two of you. In a day and age when the divorce rate is approaching 50 percent and scientists are talking seriously about a greenhouse effect that will destroy our planet, you, as a bride and groom, have chosen to go forward with the strongest affirmation of faith in your future and, therefore, in our future as well. By reaching out to each other your fingertips touch all of us, and your lovers' embrace constitutes a most eloquent refutation of those who counsel doom and gloom, defeat and despair.

The rabbis of the Talmud recount a legend that tells us that when the Israelites were frantically fleeing the pursuing Pharaoh and his army of Egyptian charioteers and came to the swirling waters of the Red Sea, they were immobilized by fear. Then, say the rabbis, an Israelite named Nachshon Ben Aminadav fearlessly jumped into the stormy waters, and at that precise moment God parted the waters so that the children of Israel could cross in safety.

In other words, miracles require courageous, determined acts of faith.

For me, you are the modern Nachshon Ben Aminadav. As you ready yourselves for your wedding day, know that you are affirming that there will be a future, a hope, a dream, for yourselves and for humankind that you will make reality.

And therefore, I as a rabbi stand from afar, in silence and with profound admiration for the miracle that you will create together, the miracle of two lives joined as one, in faith and in trust.

Rabbi Leon B. Fink

THERE ARE THOSE WHO SAY

On his wedding day, for every groom, his bride is the most beautiful woman in the world.   *Talmud*

A look may last forever.   *Heinrich Heine*

Be careful to honor your wife, for blessing enters the home only because of the wife.   *Talmud*

Set me as a seal upon thy heart.   *Song of Songs*

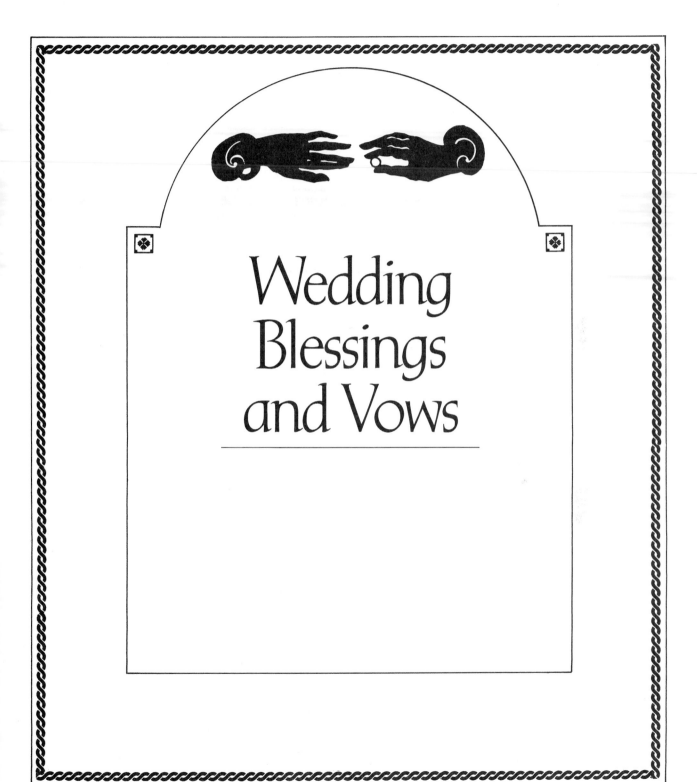

Wedding Blessings and Vows

Under the Chupah

As the couple and all those who are to join them reach the *chupah*, they face the rabbi or the individual who is to conduct the ceremony. In Jewish tradition, the rabbi does not marry the couple; the bride and groom marry each other. (Accordingly, the person who reads or chants the *berachot* (blessings) is referred to as the *mesader kiddushin*, the one who orders the service of sanctification.)

With the wedding party assembled, the rabbi reads or chants a section from Psalm 118 and/or Psalm 100 and then recites a medieval hymn. Psalm 118:26 contains a traditional Jewish blessing of welcome: "Blessed are you who come in the name of God." Psalm 100 is one of thanksgiving, expressing thanks to and praise for God. The words of the medieval hymn are: "May the One who is mighty and blessed above all bless the groom and the bride."

Circling

The bride, with an entourage, may then circle the groom three or seven times. While this custom is usually omitted from Reform ceremonies, it is a part of many Conservative and all Orthodox weddings.

The practice is based on a messianic verse from the Book of Jeremiah: "A woman shall court a man." The rabbis interpreted this to indicate that a woman should "go around" a man, hence the custom of circling.

The more usual seven circles custom has been explained in a variety of ways:

- There are seven days in a week.
- There are seven *aliyot* on Shabbat.
- The Bible says "when a man takes a wife" seven times.
- There is a mystical teaching that the bride, in circling seven times, enters seven spheres of her husband's innermost being.
- On Simchat Torah, the Torahs are carried around the synagogue seven times.

Explanations for the basis of circling three times include:

- The three times in the Book of Hosea when God, in reassuring Israel, "says": "and I will betroth you unto Me."
- A woman's three basic rights in marriage: food, clothing and sex.

Whether three or seven times, however, circling probably reflected the structure of the family in times past. The custom implicitly stated that the bride's life now revolved around her husband rather than her parents. The bride's circling also grew out of a mystical belief that, by making a ring around the groom, the woman thereby protected him from evil spirits.

Liberal Judaism moved away from circling, in part because of the practice's superstitious overtones and in part because of Reform Judaism's insistence on the absolute equality of the sexes. Still, the custom of circling remains a fascinating component of the Jewish wedding that some liberal couples choose to include, sometimes with both bride and groom circling each other.

The Betrothal Blessing

The rabbi or cantor reads or chants the *birkat erusin*, or betrothal blessing. As we have already seen, two ceremonies, originally separated by a one-year waiting period, were combined into a single rite in about the twelfth century. This next section of the service constitutes the *erusin* segment.

Erusin begins with a blessing over wine. The *birkat erusin* is recited or chanted. The bride and groom then drink from the same cup, symbolically affirming that throughout life they will experience both joy and sorrow, but always together.

The sip of wine brings life full circle for both bride and groom. At a baby boy's *berit milah* (circumcision), and at a baby girl's naming, often referred to within Reform Judaism as *berit ha-chayim* (the covenant of life), the parents recite a prayer that their child's life will include study of the Torah, deeds of loving-kindness and marriage. As part of each ceremony, the baby boy or girl is given a taste of wine.

On the wedding day, the parental prayer for marriage is realized, with a similar sip of wine confirming that happy and sacred moment.

The Ring Ceremony

In traditional ceremonies, following the betrothal blessing, the groom places the bride's ring on her right index finger. The ring is placed there because it is the most prominent location, and so that the two required witnesses can see the ring easily. This custom, originated in about the fifteenth century, also grew out of a belief that a vein in this finger runs directly to the heart. Following the ceremony, the ring is moved to the more familiar third finger of the bride's left hand. In some ceremonies, the ring is placed directly on the third finger of the left hand.

The groom then recites the legal formula of betrothal. In the presence of the two witnesses he says: *"Harei at mekudeshet li, betabaat zu, kedat Moshe ve Yisrael."* "Behold, you are consecrated unto me with this ring, according to the law of Moses and Israel."

In the Orthodox ritual, only the groom speaks. In the more liberal wings of Judaism, the bride frequently responds with the same or a different formula as she places a ring on the groom's hand.

In modern ceremonies, the bride and groom sometimes supplement the *"Harei at"* with vows that they have personally composed.

Following the exchange of vows, the ceremony of betrothal concludes. The *ketubah* is then read. The reading of the *ketubah* formally separates the betrothal and marriage ceremonies. The rabbi, a family member, a friend, or a group of friends may read the *ketubah* aloud, after which the groom hands it to the bride. It is thereafter her property. The marriage ceremony itself can now begin.

The Sheva Berachot

We now come to the heart of the marriage ceremony, called *nissuin*, the one-time culmination of a year of betrothal.

As with betrothal, *nissuin* has its own blessing over the wine. Accordingly, a second cup of wine is filled. In centuries past, European Jews often commissioned a matched pair of *kiddush* cups for a child's wedding. That custom has been embraced by many modern couples, drawn to the creations of contemporary Jewish artists.

The essence of *nissuin* is the chanting or recitation of seven blessings, the *sheva berachot*, including the blessing over wine as a symbol of joy, and the presumed fortuitous influence of the mystical number 7 to the joining of two lives as one.

The rabbi, cantor, family members or friends may read or chant the *sheva berachot*, and many couples honor those closest to them by asking them to participate in this way. This involvement is particularly appropriate in view of the *sheva berachot*'s overarching theme of creation.

The first *beracha* blesses God for creating the fruit of the vine.

The second blesses God for creating the world.

The third blesses God for creating human beings.

The fourth blesses God for having endowed us with divine potential.

The fifth blesses God for giving us the power to bring children—and thus new life—into the world.

The sixth blesses God for the joy of the wedding day, re-creating the marriage of Adam and Eve.

The seventh and final *beracha* holds out a messianic vision of a world of true peace, a world in which the bride and groom and their families may constantly rejoice in security and happiness.

The *sheva berachot* thus move from God's creation of the world to the partnership of every human being with God in seeing the potential of that world for goodness and kindness fulfilled.

Special Words

Most commonly at this point in the ceremony, the rabbi and/or a close friend, sibling or parent offers a few thoughts on the meaning and significance of love and marriage. It may take the form of a brief speech, a poem or even a song composed especially for this day.

Occasionally, more than one "charge" is presented. The bride and groom may speak to one another. In the case of a second marriage, children sometimes offer their personal good wishes.

The words spoken need not be completely serious, and gentle humor is most appropriate. The more personal the message, however, the more moving its impact.

SPECIAL WORDS
ON OUR WEDDING DAY

Who spoke: _____

The message: _____

_____

_____

_____

_____

_____

_____

_____

_____

_____

_____

_____

_____

_____

_____

_____

THE RABBIS SAY

WEDDING GIFTS

You receive many gifts on the occasion of your wedding. These gifts, from loved ones and friends, are expressions of their affection and good wishes. Enjoy them. But the greatest gifts that come to you today for your love and for its fulfillment come to you from on high, from God.

The first is the gift of family. Our Jewish heritage and values are bound up with family. Our spirituality began with the love and marriage of our first parents, Abraham and Sarah. You may be fortunate enough in your own families to have models of the kind of family commitment that enhances all the joys of life and can transform even the challenges and trials of life, when shared, into a kind of fulfillment you might otherwise never know. And you now have a beautiful opportunity to expand and strengthen your own family bonds, and thus to make your relationship all the more rich and rewarding. You, too, can be models of family bonds and commitments for generations of your family to come.

A second gift you receive is a chance for you to preserve and strengthen the Jewish tradition. You share wine from the kiddush cup during this consecration of your marriage. At this service the cup stands for our history, the songs and stories and observances that have given dignity and beauty to the life of our people and have even made our life possible. Take that heritage into your life, into your shared love, into your home, that it may become a small sanctuary. Each time, on Shabbat and holy days, at times of personal joy when you lift this cup, it can re-create this moment and thereby the affirmation of your love.

There is the gift of your own God-given abilities, the intelligence, and energy with which each of you in a unique way has been endowed. Apply these gifts not only to your work, but to your marriage above all. No work, no project so merits all your abilities as does your marriage. No endeavor is of greater consequence for the very substance and meaning and significance of your life. Nothing you can do will be more rewarding for your own happiness and fulfillment.

And finally, you have been given the divine gift of a soul that in Hebrew we call a *neshama*. From that soul comes your character: the capacity for faithfulness and responsibility. Faithfulness, responsibility to another human being, is the bedrock of any marriage. And also from the soul within us emanates the capacity for understanding, forgiveness, compassion, mercy. Since none of us is perfect, these too are the bases of any love. We never have a greater opportunity to express that image of God within us than as a husband to his wife and as a wife to her husband. Bring this gift of your special soul to your own marriage.

These are gifts from God that come to you today: the gifts of family, of the Jewish tradition, of your own capacities, of your soul. If you bring these gifts to your new home, to your marriage, then you will be truly gifted in love. And as it grows and becomes richer year by year, your love in turn will become a gift to all who love you, all who know you, all who behold you.   *Rabbi Herbert Bronstein*

THE RABBIS SAY

KADOSH AND KADOSH

The word for marriage in our tradition is *kiddushin*, from the word *kadosh*, which we usually translate as "sacred" or "holy." But in its most essential meaning, to be *kadosh* is to be "unique," like nothing else in the world.

God is *kadosh*, and every one of us, God's creatures, has his or her own *kadosh* quality, which makes each of us like no one else.

When the two of you began to become aware of that *kadosh* quality in each other, and when, by being together, you began to discover more and more the *kadosh* quality in yourselves, and when you decided that this was the way it should be—*kadosh* and *kadosh*, I and Thou, for the rest of your lives—then you had come to love and began your journey to this *chupah*.

So here you are, and you will make very practical promises to each other:

• To love, honor and cherish
• To be responsible not only to each other but also to the marriage
• To be willing to work through your differences and willing to lose an argument for the sake of the marriage
• To be willing to have a sense of humor, about yourselves and the marriage, for the sake of the marriage

But there still remains that other: that reaching out, each to confirm who the other is and who the other is capable of becoming—I and Thou, *kadosh* and *kadosh*—in a never-ending search and a never-ending discovery.

And that's what marriage is. It's the practical responsibility and the romantic search—prose and poetry uniquely entwined in the lives of two people in love.

During the ceremony you will both drink from the cup of wine, our Jewish symbol of joy. But in this cup is not only your private joy but your family's, and your friends', and your Jewish people's and your humanity's—everybody's joy belongs to you.

At the end of the ceremony you will break a glass—the shattered pieces symbolizing the tears from which no life is free. But these are not only your private tears, but your family's and friends' and the Jewish people's and humanity's.

All belong to you, because what those of us who have been married for a long time can tell you is that marriage is not for children who keep house but for grown-up human beings who take on the joys and tears of the world.

And in a private place, in a *kadosh* place of that world, just two people, the two of you, responsible to each other very practically—reaching out for each other very romantically—*kadosh* and *kadosh*—with God's blessing.

Rabbi Jack Stern

THE RABBIS SAY

THE ONENESS OF MARRIAGE

You have become united in heart and soul. The biblical idiom for marital unity is "You shall become *one* flesh." The word for "one" in Hebrew is *echad*, the same designation for the oneness of God expressed in the *shema* and the term used to describe the oneness of the Jewish people.

In a truly Jewish marriage, all of these "onenesses" converge. Oneness in a spiritual sense is not a numerical classification. It may more appropriately be referred to as "uniqueness." You are unique. There is no couple in the world like you. Your love is unique, your relationship is unique, the life you build togeth-

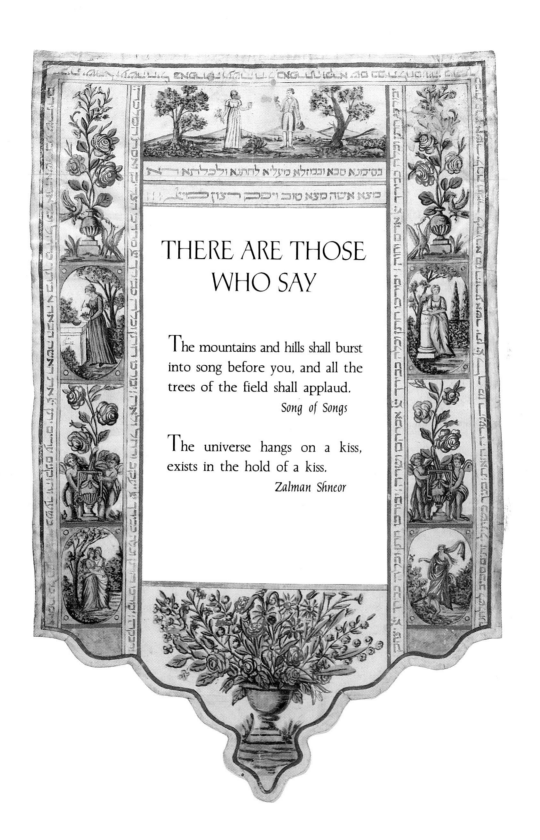

THERE ARE THOSE WHO SAY

The mountains and hills shall burst into song before you, and all the trees of the field shall applaud.

Song of Songs

The universe hangs on a kiss, exists in the hold of a kiss.

Zalman Shneor

er will be unique. This notion is also embedded in the Hebrew word for marriage, *kiddushin*, which means "holiness," and holiness means separate, distinguished, or, in essence, unique.

Your oneness, your uniqueness, is the most precious attribute of your marriage. Preserve it, guard it, fortify it. It strengthens your affinity, it invigorates your kinship, it reaffirms your consanguinity.

It also links you to God, who is also unique and holy. You have become united with God, the source of joy and blessing, who infuses creation with life and spiritual vigor. Your love for each other becomes part of God's cosmic love, without beginning or end, a love that is forgiving and appreciative, generous and compassionate.

The Jewish people whom you are now, in your oneness, a part of are also unique and holy. You are fused, thus, to the continuum of Jewish history. You are members of a people who, under the most trying conditions, have nourished and advocated those ideals that are the bedrock of our civilization—justice, virtue, humanitarianism, benevolence, charity and altruism.

It is written: "Two is better than one, but the threefold cord will not quickly be severed." The coalescence of your unity with God and the Jewish people will infuse your marriage with the sanctity that elevates, the vitality that activates, the nobility that exhilarates and the tenacity that resonates.

As a strand in the threefold cord, you are the past, the present and the future. You are the hope, the dream, the reassurance of eternity. You are the life of the universe.

Rabbi Dr. Stanley M. Wagner

THE RABBIS SAY

WISDOM BUILDS A HOME

The Jewish sages taught that "It is wisdom that builds a home."

Long ago, long before Freud, our rabbis understood that anyone could have a job, anyone could get married, anyone could build a house. But only two individuals, sensitive to one another's needs and supportive of one another's failings, could hope to create a home, a true center of love and mutual respect.

Love is a gift. It comes very rarely in life. But when it does come, we must seize it and cherish it, for true love is far more precious than any material possession we shall ever own.

Nor does love ever exist in a vacuum. Love always begets more love. And the clearest evidence of that great truth can be seen in the faces of those of your family and friends who have come together today, brought to this holy moment by your love for one another.

Our ancestors understood the power of love, and perhaps that is why God is portrayed as declaring early in the Book of Genesis: "It is not good for anyone to be alone."

Everybody needs somebody. The two of you have been blessed in finding each other. Use your gift wisely. Hold each other close. Protect and guard your love. And build your home—with wisdom.   *Rabbi Daniel B. Syme*

Breaking the Glass

The wedding ceremony concludes with the rabbi's formally pronouncing the couple husband and wife and blessing them.

The groom then breaks a glass. The custom of breaking a glass at the conclusion of the wedding began in post-talmudic times. Many scholars assert that the most primitive origins of the practice reflected a symbolic breaking of the hymen. Over the centuries, however, various interpreters have held that the breaking of the glass:

• Reminds us of the destruction of the Temple in Jerusalem.
• Teaches that, in times of joy, we must always be cognizant that life also brings sadness and sorrow.
• Drives away evil spirits, who, without this sudden noise, might spoil the occasion with some evil deed.
• Warns us that love, like glass, is fragile and must be protected.

Many couples purchase a special glass to be broken at their ceremony. Increasingly, however, a light bulb rather than a glass is used.

Jewish custom does not specifically prescribe a drinking glass, and a light bulb makes much more noise. The glass or bulb is wrapped tightly in a linen napkin before it is shattered. In some modern ceremonies, the bride as well as the groom breaks a glass.

Everyone present yells "Mazal tov" or "Siman tov!" These two Hebrew phrases convey a sense of "congratulations." Ashkenazic Jews usually yell "Mazal tov," while Sephardic Jews yell "Siman tov." Interestingly, both phrases derive from astrology. Mazal literally means "planet"; siman, "omen." Thus, either exclamation amounts to wishing the new couple a "good horoscope," in addition to expressing a warm sentiment.

While many Orthodox couples refrain from doing so out of a sense of modesty, most brides and grooms embrace and kiss before leaving the chupah. They then leave the sanctuary, or place of the ceremony, and retire to a separate room for a few moments alone before joining their friends and family. This practice, called yichud or "privacy," enables couples who have fasted to break their fast together and, above all, to share the significance of a new family in the household of Israel.

HOW WE FELT AT THE END
OF OUR WEDDING CEREMONY

THERE ARE THOSE WHO SAY

WINE, CANOPY, RING AND GLASS

I.   Pour my cup of wine with thine
into one empty vessel
Fill it with drink of laughter, song, and love
Drink together a new mixture
our wines like our lives intermingled
Fusion without coercion
merger without loss of individuality
a curious admixture
two into one
one into two
union without subtraction
Singularity that multiplies.

II.   Four separate poles of the wedding canopy
an extraordinary geometry
The pillars stand apart
Too close the curtain collapses
Too far it will not hold
Let there be space in our togetherness
the distance that brings together.

III.   Take this ring unbejeweled
as simple as love
not blinded by the glitter of opulence
Take this ring
a circle not to exclude
but to embrace family and friends
An expanding encirclement
whose outer rim touches the hem of God.

IV.   This glass we break
      symbol of fragility
      However strong we appear
      we are vulnerable
      to words that hurt and silences that pain
      Gentle now, soft now, tender now
      we two are fragile
      This broken glass
      symbol of a shattered society, a temple unbuilt
      Poverty, homelessness, rage in the
      world about us
      We blessed with God's gift to creation
      pledge ourselves to bind up the bruises
      make what fragmented lives
      Rejoice the world that rejoices us.

 V.   Love more powerful than death
      heals, binds, cures, cares, resurrects,
      where there is love there is life
      where there is love there is hope.

VI.   Rejoice with me our sacred friendship
      the birth of a new syntax
      a metamorphosis
      from me and mine
      to we and ours
      a new word is born
      a new world created
      a new beginning
      a new promise

VII. In seven days a world is formed
      with seven benedictions a world is renewed.

Rabbi Harold M. Schulweis

Celebration

The Wedding Party

Extravagant wedding parties were never encouraged in Judaism. Indeed, a number of Jewish communities over the centuries (including modern Israel) actually passed legislation limiting their opulence. Though Jewish custom discourages ostentation, the wedding banquet remains a cause for great joy and celebration, filled with music and dancing and fulfilling the *mitzvah* to "make the bride and groom merry."

The Talmud asserted that a marriage should be celebrated for seven days, with the *sheva berachot* recited every day. The Jewish law requiring a *minyan* for recitation of these blessings underscores the status of the wedding as a major community event.

The suggested seven-day celebration derives from the Book of Genesis. Laban prepared a feast for Jacob's wedding. After substituting Leah for Rachel, on the grounds that the eldest daughter had to be married first, Laban sought to assuage Jacob's anger by telling him: "Fulfill the *week* of this one, and we will give you the other also for the service, which you shall serve with me yet seven other years." Laban's use of the word "week" became the justification for the seven days of rejoicing.

Whatever the rationale, the wedding party is most often a time of unbridled happiness. The meal should begin with a *motzi*, a blessing, usually over a large *chalah*. The meal, or *seudat mitzvah*—a meal that follows observance of a commandment—should conclude with *birkat hamazon*, the traditional blessing thanking God for food.

The Jewish wedding party itself, featuring dancing, singing, plentiful quantities of food, toasts and tributes, often lasts into the wee hours of the night.

From the long-gone *shtetl* of Eastern Europe to the present, *klezmer* musicians kept guests dancing to the point of exhaustion, while the *badchan*, a sort of Eastern European master of ceremonies, convulsed them with laughter. After all, the bride and groom are treated in Jewish tradition as a king and queen, and therefore are entitled to regal entertainment.

During the Italian Renaissance, guests created poems and plays for the newly married couple. Today, friends often prepare skits, slide shows or videotapes for the party. Contemporary music is the norm for wedding parties today, but Jewish couples frequently engage musicians who also include *klezmer*, Yiddish, Israeli and chasidic songs in their repertoire.

At some point in the party, even as a king and queen sit on royal thrones, the bride and groom are often seated on chairs and lifted high above the dance floor, carried on the shoulders of friends who wish them well. As the Talmud teaches: "The real merit in attending a wedding lies in the congratulations offered to the bride and groom."

MEMORIES OF OUR
WEDDING PARTY

The most beautiful moment

_____
_____
_____
_____
_____
_____

The most touching moment

_____
_____
_____
_____
_____
_____

The funniest moment

_____
_____
_____
_____
_____
_____

PHOTOS FROM
OUR WEDDING DAY

GIFT REGISTRY

Gift   From

_____

_____

_____

_____

_____

_____

_____

_____

_____

_____

_____

_____

_____

_____

_____

_____

_____

_____

_____

GIFT REGISTRY

Gift   From

_____

_____

_____

_____

_____

_____

_____

_____

_____

_____

_____

_____

_____

_____

_____

_____

_____

_____

_____

_____

Starting Your
Jewish Home

Ritual Objects

It is never too soon to begin to create your own Jewish home. As you sort through your wedding gifts, see if you have received some or all of the items listed below. If so, wonderful. If not, consider a visit to one or more stores that specialize in Jewish ritual objects and begin to build your own collection of Judaica.

Of course, the first thing you should do after returning from your honeymoon is to join a synagogue if you do not already belong to one. The synagogue can serve as your extended Jewish family, and ultimately for your children as well. As the central institution of Jewish life, the synagogue deserves your support and participation.

Many synagogues themselves have Judaica shops. Members of the committee in charge, often the sisterhood, can be a wonderful resource in obtaining the objects you want and need.

A Mezuzah

The Hebrew word *mezuzah* means "doorpost." According to tradition, a *mezuzah* is to be affixed to the doorpost at the entrance to your home, as well as to the entrance of each interior room, except for bathrooms. Many Jews, however, have a *mezuzah* only on the front doorpost. The *mezuzah* itself consists of a small scroll of parchment, called a *klaf*, on which are written

two biblical passages from the Book of Deuteronomy. This scroll is then inserted into a wooden, plastic or metal casing, which is often quite beautiful in design. A *mezuzah* distinguishes a Jewish home. It is a visible sign to all who enter that a sense of Jewish identity and commitment exists within your household.

You will find a host of casings for the *mezuzah*, from the simplest to the most elaborate. You may even choose to design and create your own. An authentic *klaf*, however, should be purchased and placed inside. The *mezuzah* should then be affixed to the doorpost in a ceremony called *Chanukat Ha-Bayit,* "the dedication of a home." This is a family ceremony, attended by all family members. Consult your rabbi for the appropriate blessings.

Shabbat Candlesticks

Your Shabbat candlesticks were probably a gift from your parents or a member of your family. In some families, Shabbat candlesticks are passed down from generation to generation. If not, they should be one of your first purchases. Shabbat candlesticks may be of any shape or size, with silver, brass or wood being the most commonly used materials. North American and Israeli artisans have created Shabbat candlesticks of great beauty in recent times. Most Jewish bookstores have a nice selection.

THERE ARE THOSE
WHO SAY

Except the Holy One build the house, they labor in vain that build it.   *Psalm 127*

And though these shattering walls are thin
May they be strong to keep hate out
And hold love in.   *Louis Untermeyer*

Kiddush Cup

Even as you drank from a cup of wine on your wedding day, so you will chant the *kiddush* as a family on Friday night as Shabbat begins and on the various festivals of the Jewish calendar year. Many couples use the cup from their wedding ceremony as the *kiddush* cup for their home. Like Shabbat candlesticks, *kiddush* cups are often passed down as heirlooms from parents to children. As children are born, it is often the custom to purchase a new cup in honor of the new family member, which in turn becomes the child's own *kiddush* cup for life. There is no prescribed form or design for the *kiddush* cup. Any cup or glass may be used, the only traditional requirement being that it contains the capacity for at least 3.3 ounces of wine.

A Chalah Plate, a Knife and a Cover

On Shabbat and other holidays, Jewish families recite the *motzi*, the blessing over bread, over a special *chalah* loaf. You may purchase *chalah* plates and knives, as well as elegant *chalah* covers. The *chalah* cover, in particular, teaches an important Jewish value. On Shabbat, the Shabbat candles are placed in beautiful candlesticks and the wine is held up in a lovely *kiddush* cup. While the blessings over them are being recited, the *chalah* lies alone and ignored on the table. Long ago, the rabbis, seeing this, decreed that the *chalah* should be covered, lest its feelings be hurt by its seemingly secondary status. One rabbi said: "This teaches us concern for the feelings even of inanimate objects. And if this is the case, how much more so should we be concerned about the feelings of human beings." Thus, the *chalah* cover becomes a symbol and a lesson in human dignity.

Such *chalah* sets may be purchased at most Judaica shops.

Havdalah Set

Havdalah, a Hebrew word meaning "division" or "separation," is also the name of the beautiful ritual that formally ends Shabbat. The ritual objects utilized in the *havdalah* service include a *kiddush* cup, a spice box and a special braided *havdalah* candle with two or more wicks.

The spice box has inspired Jewish artisans for many centuries. According to rabbinic legend, each Jew receives an additional soul on Shabbat. At the end of Shabbat, the extra soul departs. The smelling of fragrant spices thus became a symbolic way of refreshing the soul and compensating the individual for the loss of extra spiritual strength. Spice boxes are usually made of silver or wood, though tradition prescribes no special form for them. Indeed, many families make their own.

You may use your own *kiddush* cup for *Havdalah*. When you visit your local Judaica shop, however, ask to see the numerous *havdalah* sets available.

Passover Seder Plate and Haggadah

Passover is perhaps the most beloved Jewish holiday. The centerpiece of the seder observance is the seder plate itself, which has sections designed to hold the various seder symbols: a roasted shank bone, *matzah*, bitter herbs, a roasted egg, a vegetable such as parsley, charoset and a dish of salt water. Passover seder plates have been created in every land in which Jews have lived throughout the centuries and are made of every conceivable material. Silver, crockery, china, glass and other materials have all been adorned with Hebrew lettering and multicolored artistic illustrations of this great story of the deliverance from slavery to freedom of the Jewish people.

The Haggadah, which contains the order of the service, should be in every Jewish home in sufficient quantities for the size of the seder that you intend to conduct. Literally hundreds of Haggadahs are available in Jewish bookstores, and often in commercial bookstores as well. You will have to select the Haggadah that is best for your home and your family.

Other Objects for the Passover Seder

In addition to the seder plate and the Haggadah, many families beautify the seder service with a special *kiddush* cup for the prophet Elijah, a linen bag divided into three sections for the three *matzahs* traditionally placed on the seder table, and artistically designed dishes for individual seder symbols. Many Judaica shops, particularly those in Israel, have a wide selection of such items.

Chanukah Menorah

The Chanukah menorah, *chanukiyah* in Hebrew, is a must for every Jewish home. This nine-branched candelabrum, formalized as a Chanukah symbol in about the first century c.e., has one branch for each day of the holiday and a ninth branch for the *shamash*, or "servant" light. In ancient times, oil was used in the menorah. Over time, candles were substituted for the oil.

The Chanukah menorah may be made of any material—metal, wood, porcelain, or a host of others. Whatever your artistic preference, you can be certain that there is a Chanukah menorah exactly right for your home.

Apples and Honey Dish for Rosh Hashanah

On the eve of each Jewish New Year, Rosh Hashanah, it is customary to dip apples in honey and eat them together as we wish one another a sweet new year of health and happiness. Jewish artists have designed apples and honey sets for Rosh Hashanah. Though they are not as commonly seen in many Judaica shops, if you look carefully and find one, it is well worth the effort.

A Sukah, a Lulav and an Etrog

The holiday of Sukot, the Jewish fall harvest festival, offers an opportunity to those who are ambitious and fairly proficient in construction.

1.

2.

3.

4.

5.

6.

7.

1. Matzah cover, Hungary, 19th century
2. Sabbath cloth, United States, 19th century.
3. Mezuzah case, United States, 1955.
4. Sarajevo Haggadah, Spain, 14th century.
5. Challah tray, knife, and salt cellar, United States, 1982.
6. Candlesticks, Russia, 19th century.
7. Hanukkah lamp, Morocco, 19th century.
8. Seder plate, Italy, 19th century.

8.

It is customary for Jews to build a *sukah* in their yard or porch in which they recite special prayers, eat meals and invite guests to join them for meals during the holiday. The *sukah*, a structure that generally has at least three walls, may be constructed of any material, generally canvas, wood or metal. The roof must be temporary, covered with loose branches from trees or other vegetation. According to tradition, this roof covering, *sechach*, should give shade and yet allow those in the *sukah* to view the stars through the roof at night. The *sukah* may be decorated by hanging fruit, putting posters on the walls and even laying carpet on the floor. For those who are less adept at creating structures, prefabricated *sukot* are available from a number of Judaica supply houses. In larger communities, you may even engage individuals who specialize in putting the *sukah* together.

As Sukot approaches, you will also want to purchase a *lulav* and *etrog* for the recitation of the appropriate blessings within the *sukah*. *Lulav* is a Hebrew word meaning "palm branch," *etrog*, a Hebrew word meaning "citron." The *lulav* and *etrog* are generally purchased from a central community source. In larger cities you may even find a *lulav* and *etrog* market, such as exists on the Lower East Side of Manhattan, in New York City, just prior to the holiday. If you wish, you may even purchase a beautiful container for your *etrog*, another product of new artistic expression growing out of ancient Jewish custom.

A Jewish Home Library

Every Jewish home must have a library of Jewish books. We Jews are the people of the book, and there is no end to the volumes with which you may choose to grace the bookshelves of your new home. You should have prayer books, a Torah translation with commentaries, books on Jewish holidays and life cycle events, books on Jewish history and books on Jewish themes of all sorts. Find a good Jewish bookstore and get to know the owner. He or she can be a valuable resource in helping you build a Jewish home library.

RITUAL OBJECTS
IN OUR JEWISH HOME

Ritual object   When and where acquired

As You Begin Your Life Together

THERE ARE THOSE WHO SAY

Shalom and *mazal tov* on your marriage. Soon now, after the excitement dies down, you will face the reality of new beginnings—a new family to forge a link in the 4000-year chain of Judaism.

You still retain the love and protection of your respective families, but you must now proceed on your own. How should you do this? Perhaps a brief review of my three families might be helpful.

I came from a large family; my parents were both born in Russia. My father had an excellent Jewish education. My mother was the local "folk" doctor—a godsend during the Depression and probably one of the reasons I became a physician. I always followed her example to treat anyone I saw, regardless of his or her ability to pay for medical care.

Though we were Orthodox, we rarely went to Shabbat services. My father explained that Judaism was a religion for life. If we closed on Saturday, we could not survive. He often told me that while he was in the Russian Army, he ate the nonkosher food given to him so that he could live.

Ours was a family of eleven children. We were close and supportive. We enjoyed the Jewish holidays, and Friday was our favorite day. The house smelled of fresh-baked *chalah*. On Friday night my mother lit the Shabbat candles, and we ate *chalah* and drank wine.

As I grew up in this "first" family, I learned many lessons, three of which especially have left their mark.

First, *Tzedakah*. No matter how desperate our circumstances were, there was always some less fortunate person who needed help.

The next precept, certainly related to *tzedakah*, was never to refuse to feed a hungry person. Once, one of my sisters turned down a hungry man. A few moments later, she became so remorseful that she ran three blocks to bring the man back to feed him.

I also learned about civil rights. My father had rented a small shop to a black man. That evening the upstairs tenant came to complain. "Either he goes or we do." My father responded: "You are welcome to leave at any time."

I finished high school, worked in a factory, went to night school, finally completed college and applied for medical school. To my chagrin, even though I had graduated first in my class, I, the only Jew to apply, was rejected. The irony was that I had tutored the other applicants in biochemistry so that they could pass and be eligible for medical school.

My family supported me, and I was ultimately accepted at our state university and then at the University of Tennessee at Memphis. I graduated with both an M.D. degree and a commission in the United States Army.

I came home, started training and married my college sweetheart. The marriage, like yours, was performed under a *chupah*, with the same vows and blessings. So began my second family.

We had a son, and soon thereafter I was called to military service in Germany. I returned after two years and then tragedy struck. My wife, aged twenty-five, died of leukemia. I was devastated. How could I continue training and also raise a young child? I was a ship without a rudder. My family provided support and love, and I moved in with one of my sisters.

After several months, I began living again. I met and dated a lovely, caring social worker whom I later married. My third family again began under the *chupah*. Continuity. The same blessings and vows were repeated.

My wife and I decided to learn more about Judaism. We read books and joined study groups. My wife became active in both Jewish and secular organizations. I became active in the synagogue. We continued to learn about our wonderful Jewish heritage.

My third family grew. We now have four sons, four daughters and eleven grandchildren. We are a Jewish family who is proud of our tradition, very close and all good friends.

We sent our children to Hebrew school and kept Jewish books at home for them to read. I guess most of the teaching was done by example. We wanted to continue the 4000-year chain of Judaism.

Our Judaism was particularly meaningful at our Passover seders. We felt the closeness of Jews everywhere, celebrating with us our freedom from slavery. All Israel was united.

As I look back on my three families, on the happiness and joy, the tragedy and illness, the strength that we derived from one another even in the darkest days of despair, I realize how much there is in life to be grateful for. You are blessed indeed if you have a partner, a friend, a mate to share whatever life brings in devotion and mutual respect and affection as Jews.

So, my young friends, go forth from your wedding ceremony as proud Jews. Make for yourselves a wonderful life together. Raise a family, and hold it close and dear. If you follow the teachings and embrace the values of our faith, you will find life to be more meaningful. May God bless and keep you.

Dr. Aaron Hendin

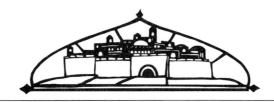

THE RABBIS SAY

When I was a boy, most stories ended the same way: "They were married, and they lived happily ever after." It was taken for granted that marriage would lead to eternal bliss. That's not true anymore. Many stories today have an entirely different conclusion. The rate of divorce has risen alarmingly.

Various reasons have been given for this sudden collapse of the marital institution. It is not my purpose to consider the causes of the *breakdown*. Rather, let me direct your attention to how a marriage can be *built*.

Every profession requires preparation. To be a doctor, a lawyer, or an engineer requires years of schooling and many hours of instruction before the diploma is presented.

What preparation is required for marriage? The answer is, nothing except sufficient money to pay for a marriage license.

If you were setting out on a lengthy journey by automobile, you would certainly secure a road map. You would want to know which roads to avoid and which detours to follow. What I would like to do is to provide you with a road map that, hopefully, will assist you in surmounting those obstacles that invariably arise in most marriages and guide you to a more loving and lasting relationship.

Basically, most marriage authorities agree that the ideal marriage consists of four relationships. As I touch on each one, ask yourself how much of the specific relationship you have already achieved and how much you may yet have to attain.

The first, and probably the most important, relationship is "friend–friend." What does this mean? If you are *his* best friend, you will never embarrass or criticize him publicly. When you are alone, you can tell him what his faults are (in a *kind* way), but never publicly—and you have a right to expect the same from him.

If you are *her* best friend, she never has to worry about where you are or who you are with, because you would never do anything to destroy her faith in you—and you have a right to expect the same from her. Thus, you never have to ask each other "Where were you?", "Why are you late?", or "Where did you go?" because, without faith and trust in each other, your marriage is built on quicksand.

In addition, the friend–friend relationship involves empathy. This is illustrated by Tolstoy's story of two peasants who are talking. The first peasant says: "You tell me that you love me. If so, do you know what makes me cry?" "How should I know what makes you cry?" responds the other. The first peasant replies: "If you don't know what makes me cry, you don't love me."

What a remarkable insight into a meaningful relationship! "Do you know what makes me cry?" Do you know what causes pain to the other? And if so, do you try to avoid that kind of behavior? When two married people describe the other as "my best friend," they are well on the road to marital happiness.

The second relationship is "lover–lover." It is rather disheartening, in our sex-drenched society, to hear how few married couples have a happy love relationship. So many times I have heard young brides complain, "I feel so used," or "When my husband comes home and uses affectionate or endearing terms, I know that he is expecting to have sex. That's the only time that he treats me with warmth and caring." It is important, therefore, for every couple to read some books on the art of loving, whereby they learn to understand each other's moods and to value each other's needs. In Judaism, sex is beautiful. God gave us bodies to use—but not for our selfish use. The blending of our bodies can bring us closer together, not only physically but also emotionally and spiritually.

The third relationship is "father–daughter." Every woman has a little girl in her. She expects two things from her "daddy:" First, there is

praise. Consider the woman who spends over an hour getting ready to go out for the evening. As she comes out of the bedroom, her husband looks at his watch and angrily exclaims, "We're going to be late," instead of saying, "You look so beautiful." Praise is one of the vitamins essential for a happy matrimonial diet. The husband who says to his wife, "I was very proud of you when my family met you," or the husband who presents his wife with a gift on some occasion other than her birthday or their anniversary and tells her how fortunate he is that she came into his life, is certain to have a wife who will grow more radiant with the passing of time.

In addition to praise, there is the element of protectiveness. He comes home, and she tells him that several bills arrived that morning. She is worried about their economic well-being. What is his reaction? If he is truly a man (and not a boy), he will put his arms around her and say, "I don't want you to worry. Later tonight, we'll sit down and work it out together." In those moments, she realizes that when her own strength falters, she can always look to him for strength.

Finally, there is the "mother–son" relationship. This relationship represents unconditional love. As long as a mother is alive, no matter who we are, regardless of what we have achieved or failed at, we know that there is one person who loves us, who believes in us. I recall being in Florida when a murderer was about to be executed. He confessed to having killed more than thirty people. The police believed that he had killed more than twice that number. The day before the execution, his mother was interviewed on television. When questioned about her son, she said, "The police and the judge have made a terrible mistake. My son is such a gentle, such a kind boy. He could never kill anyone."

That is unconditional love. That's why grown men cry when their mothers die, because they know that no one will ever love them or defend them as did their mothers. Of course, not many wives can ever reach that stage, but it remains a goal to strive for. A man who knows that waiting at home is someone who really loves him and cares about him will always be anxious to get home to a sanctuary of caring and concern.

We sometimes speak of the "miracle of love." In a sense, it *is* a miracle. Two people from entirely different backgrounds, from completely diverse environments, will meet and, under the magic spell of love, entrust their hearts to each other. Yes, *falling* in love is a miracle. But *staying* in love is not. It requires commitment, compassion, consecration. It involves the four relationships that I have outlined above. If husband and wife strive for these ideals, they will create for themselves a safe and sure road map leading to a better and brighter future. They will transform their house into a home—a miniature sanctuary worthy even for God to dwell therein.

Rabbi M. Robert Syme

THERE ARE THOSE WHO SAY

Marriage is something special. I guess you have to deserve it. *Clifford Odets*

Memories are all we truly own. *Jewish Folk Saying*

Love turns one person into two and two into one. *Isaac Abravanel*

Entreat me not to leave thee, or to return from following after thee. For whither thou goest I will go, and where thou lodgest I will lodge. Thy people shall be my people, and thy God my God. *Book of Ruth*

AFTER A TIME—PERHAPS

After a time, the anxiety that had built exponentially during the weeks and months preceding the wedding passed. The long discussions over who would stand beside whom and who could be seated with whom were concluded. All survived. The bride and groom were beautiful; the ceremony was all they had hoped for. The parents cried and then laughed with joy, and everyone celebrated with full hearts.

The family went home. Thank-you notes were sent. However, to say that everything returned to normal would not be accurate. Jonathan and Laurie spent their first two years trying to figure out what "normal" meant.

And then Jeremy was born. They were not a young couple, and both felt deep gratitude for the relative ease of his conception and birth. To them, Jeremy was proof of the miraculous. The world became new to them as they witnessed Jeremy's firsts: his first smile, his discovery of his fingers and toes, his first steps; his first autumn, his first winter and his first spring.

When Jeremy was one week old, Laurie turned to Jonathan and said, "Before the wedding, the rabbi asked us if we were committed to keeping a Jewish home."

"Uh huh," nodded Jonathan.

"And we said we would," continued Laurie.

"I remember," said Jonathan. "What's your point?"

"What did the rabbi mean? What did we agree to? I mean, after all, now we have Jeremy..."

Jonathan was silent. They both sat quietly, looking at the baby.

"Let's call my parents," said Jonathan.

That Friday night, they began lighting Shabbat candles. The next week, they added wine and *chalah*. When Jeremy was a month old, they began blessing him as part of their ceremony.

Some practices they learned from Jonathan's parents; others they read about in books. Many came straight from their hearts.

When Jeremy was almost two years of age, they invited me to their home for dinner. Jeremy danced, climbed and played peek-a-boo all evening, still the primary wonder in his parents' home. Soon it grew dark. Time for bed.

"Bedtime, Jeremy," said Laurie, picking him up and giving him a big hug.

Jonathan walked over, holding a quarter in one hand, a box in the other.

"Tzukah!" shouted Jeremy.

"That's right, *tzedakah*," said Jonathan.

Jeremy squealed with pleasure and then, with great concentration, brought the quarter toward the slot on the top of the box.

"He puts *all* the loose change he can find into the *tzedakah* box. It's his game. That's what he thinks money is for," whispered Laurie.

The coin fell into the box.

"Good, Jermy!" shouted Jeremy.

"Good job, Jeremy!" said Laurie, giving him a hug.

"Nice work," said Jonathan, kissing his fingers and his toes.

The nighttime ritual complete, the two of them put Jeremy to bed. In the sweet moments that followed, Jeremy fell asleep.

Rabbi Deborah Ruth Bronstein

SOURCES

American Jewish Archives: pp. 72, 119.

The Archives of The Arizona Jewish Historical Society, Greater Phoenix Chapter: p. 53(bottom right).

Copyright 1991 ARS, N.Y./ADAGP: pp. 114, 142.

Beth Hatefutsoth—Photo Archive: pp. 51(center left), 70(bottom, courtesy of Gershon Ben Oren, Jerusalem), 78.

CJC National Archives: p. 53(top left).

Given in memory of sister, Jennie Berlint, by Ethel Baras-Benjamin and Dr. Edgar R. Cofeld, Judaic Museum of Temple Beth Zion: p. 35.

Renate Dollinger, Salem, OR: pp. 64, 116.

Eretz Israel Museum, Tel Aviv, Israel: pp. 7, 8, 15, 83(top), 86, 143.

The Fenster Museum of Jewish Art, Tulsa, OK: pp. 20(center right), 32(from the Oklahoma Jewish Archive), 61(bottom), 88(2.), 89(8.), 118, 151.

Giraudon/Art Resource, NY: p. 142.

From the collection of the Hebrew Union College Skirball Museum: pp. 27(Marvin Rand, photographer), 45, 99(Marvin Rand, photographer), 110(bottom, Lelo Carter, photographer), 117(Marvin Rand, photographer).

Dr. Aaron Hendin: p. 88(3.).

I.P.P.A. Tel Aviv: p. 97.

Israel Museum, Jerusalem: pp. 53(top right), 89(6. & 7.), 139 (8., David Harris photographer), 149(David Harris photographer).

Archives of the Jewish Federation of Nashville, TN: p. 51(top left).

Collection Jewish Historical Museum, Amsterdam: p. 132.

Jewish Historical Society of Western Canada: pp. 16(top, JHS 2309, JM 2020), 53(bottom left, JHS 1834, JM 266a).

Jewish Museum/Art Resource, N.Y.: pp. 39, 46, 63, 69, 94, 138(2.), 139(6. & 7.).

Jewish National and University Library, Jerusalem: p. 106 (bottom).

Courtesy of the Library of The Jewish Theological Seminary of America: pp. 2, 25, 30, 83(bottom), 111(bottom).

Judah Magnes Museum: p. 109(bottom).

Victor Laredo, New York, NY: p. 104.

Courtesy of the Leo Baeck Institute, NY: p. 40.

The Byron Collection, Museum of the City of New York: p. 124(top right, #1351; bottom, #1353).

Jewish Division, The New York Public Library. Astor, Lenox and Tilden Foundations: p. 9.

Philadelphia Jewish Archives Center: pp. 93, 124(top left).

Chava Wolpert Richard, New York, NY: p. 139(5.).

From the collection of Rabbi William Rosenthall: pp. 10, 20(top, center left, bottom), 36(bottom), 42.

The Schocken Institute for Jewish Research, Jerusalem: p. 13.

Al Silverstein, Bronx, NY: p. 85.

University of Washington Libraries, Jewish Archives Project: p. 16(bottom, neg. # UW993).

Wolfson Museum at Hechal Shlomo, Jerusalem: p. 138(1.).

From Yeshiva University Museum's exhibition: pp. 56 (bottom, *Ashkenaz: The German Jewish Heritage*), 138(3., *The Jewish Wedding*).

PAPERCUT ARTISTS AND CALLIGRAPHERS

Lynne Avadenka, Huntington Woods, MI: pp. 4, 76, 102(top), 113, 146.

Avraham Cohen, Baltimore, MD: p. 89(5.).

Galia Goodman, Durham, NC: Border design on pages 22, 47, 54, 69, 72, 73, 93, 103, 144, 145, 149. Detail taken from larger work.

Jay Greenspan, New York, NY: pp. 81, 88(1. & 4.), 135.

Naomi Hordes, Silver Spring, MD: pp. 43(top), 103.

Dan Howarth, Baltimore, MD: p. 101.

Greta Kessler, Stamford, CT: p. 51(bottom).

Jack Tetalman, Cleveland Heights, OH: pp. iii, 51(top right).

Jean Tetalman, Cleveland Heights, OH: pp. vii, 1(top), 11(center figures), 24, 29(bottom), 33(top), 34, 49, 65(top), 70(top), 79(top), 84, 95, 105(top), 107, 108(bottom), 120, 125(top).

Jack and Jean Tetalman, Cleveland Heights, OH: p. 21.

Tsirl Waletzky, Riverdale, NY: pp. 3, 11(top), 22, 54(bottom), 71(bottom), 77, 80(bottom), 148.